THE DON'T SWEAT GUIDE
TO YOUR JOB SEARCH

T0382430

Other books by the editors of Don't Sweat Press

The Don't Sweat Affirmations
The Don't Sweat Guide for Couples
The Don't Sweat Guide for Graduates
The Don't Sweat Guide for Grandparents
The Don't Sweat Guide for Parents
The Don't Sweat Guide for Moms
The Don't Sweat Guide for Weddings
The Don't Sweat Guide to Golf
The Don't Sweat Stories
The Don't Sweat Guide to Travel
The Don't Sweat Guide to Weight Loss
The Don't Sweat Guide to Taxes
The Don't Sweat Guide for Dads
The Don't Sweat Guide to Retirement
The Don't Sweat Guide for Teachers
The Don't Sweat Guide for Newlyweds
The Don't Sweat Guide to Cooking
The Don't Sweat Guide to Your New Home
The Don't Sweat Guide to Holidays
The Don't Sweat Guide to Entertaining
The Don't Sweat Guide to Your Finances
The Don't Sweat Guide to Pregnancy

THE DON'T SWEAT GUIDE
TO YOUR JOB SEARCH

Finding a Career
You Really Love

By the Editors of Don't Sweat Press
Foreword by Richard Carlson, Ph.D.

New York

ISBN: 1-4013-0760-4

Hyperion books are available for special promotions and premiums.
For details contact Michael Rentas, Manager, Inventory and Premium Sales,
Hyperion, 77 West 66th Street, 11th floor, New York, New York 10023,
or call 212-456-0133.

FIRST EDITION

Contents

Foreword

What a perfect time to read this book! Today, more than at any time in recent history, searching for a job has become a reality for an enormous number of people. Few things are potentially more stressful.

I've always believed that the more stressful a situation is, the more important it is to remain calm and in the eye of the storm. The reason this is true is because when you're calm, you're able to see the bigger picture, keep your perspective, be far more creative, and see opportunities when they present themselves. You're also able to avoid some of the problems that occur when you're stressed out, such as overreacting to criticism, acting defensive, taking things personally, feeling defeated, quitting too soon, and turning people off with a defeatist attitude!

People love to be around those who are calm, assured, and happy. Those who are in the position of hiring employees are no different. One of the intangible secrets of the universe is that happiness is extremely contagious. People can't help themselves;

11

when you're happy, they will want to help you. Even if they can't hire you, they may be able to steer you in a helpful direction!

The editors of Don't Sweat Press have done a fabulous job at creating a helpful, inspiring guide to searching for a job. This book is filled with great ideas which will help you remain calm, creative, wise, and inspired all throughout the process. It will help you or someone you care about to find that ideal position that you've been searching for. It will jumpstart you if you're just beginning, keep you on track if you're on your way, or get you over that last hurdle if you're just about there!

I've known many people over the past several years who have had a tough time searching for a job. I wish this book had been available sooner, because if it had, I would have given it to each of them as a gift. I hope you find it useful, and most importantly, that you find the perfect job just for you. I send you my love and best wishes.

Richard Carlson
Benicia, California, 2004

THE DON'T SWEAT GUIDE
TO YOUR JOB SEARCH

1.

A Challenging, Exciting Quest

If you're about to launch a job search, you're on the edge of one of the most challenging and exciting periods of your professional and personal life. Right now, you're painfully aware of the challenges that being without a position and regular income pose. However, there is another way to view your situation. This can be a stimulating time, a moment of self-discovery—though admittedly, you may have a hard time seeing the excitement.

Certainly, this isn't exactly where you wanted to be. Anyone who blithely tries (in a misguided but well-intended effort) to cheer you up by suggesting that you're better off without your old job hasn't been in your position. You've suffered a blow to your ego, and the uncertainty about your financial situation isn't helping matters.

Don't let the negatives obscure the brighter aspects of the journey ahead. Think about your old job. Was it satisfying in every regard, or did inefficient operations, overbearing supervisors, and unpleasant work conditions produce frustrations that had been building for months or years? You're beyond those frustrations now, with an opportunity to identify a better work environment. Did your former position fully utilize your skills, or did you feel that your abilities were stifled, sacrificed perhaps to outmoded work rules or silly turf battles? If that was the case, you're free now to seek a position that will utilize your talents. Did your previous employer offer you adequate upward mobility, or were you buried in an unsuitable, unrewarding box? You're out of the box now, unencumbered, circling, and soaring as high as you can.

A job search provides you with uncommon control over your destiny—perhaps more than you're used to exercising. You—and no one else—will select which job characteristics are important to you, which employment availabilities you'll pursue, which interviews you'll schedule, and which offers you'll consider and ultimately accept. If relocation and returning to school for new skills are issues, they're choices that *you* will make.

When you were working, your future always seemed to be in the hands of others. Now, that same twist of fate that wrenched you from the workforce has placed your future back in your hands. Shaping your own future—that's the thrill of a job search, a thrill you're about to experience.

2.

The Glass Is Half-Full

Much like beauty, a job search is in the eyes of the beholder. Some see it as a nerve-jangling ordeal that leads to dead ends, rejection, and a series of demanding, unsatisfying choices. Others view a job search as a compelling adventure that produces meetings with interesting people, fruitful contacts, expanded knowledge and skills, and fascinating discoveries.

Is the glass half-empty or half-full? Perception can become a self-fulfilling prophecy. Knowing how difficult the mission is and expecting the worst, "half-empty" searchers with a negative attitude don't put their best foot forward and achieve less than they otherwise could. Each disappointment reinforces their gloom, so they never have a chance to break the sour cycle. "Half-full" people, on the other hand, expect great things to happen. Their attitude is reflected in an enthusiasm that *makes* those great things happen. That, in turn, reinforces their positive approach.

Half-empty or half-full? It's an important determination for you at the very outset of your search, as it can help influence both the quality

17

and productivity of your quest. If you drift into your search without taking a stand on your attitude, you'll miss a unique opportunity to set the proper tone.

Make this decision consciously. If your personality is naturally buoyant, you won't have any trouble selecting the proper mind set. Even if you're more disposed to caution, however, you can and should make a deliberate decision to remain upbeat—no matter what disappointments your search might bring.

Remind yourself time and again about the rewarding payoffs ahead. Treat all experiences—even those that don't immediately advance your goal—as information to file away for later use. Let your job search glass always be half-full. It won't be long before you top it off—and toast your promising new position.

3.

Seeking Your First Job

The search for your first job will be one of the most exhilarating episodes of your life. You're ready to join the working world and implement everything that you've learned through your years of education. You're about to make your own way in the world, even as you begin making a concrete contribution to the social good. Congratulations on achieving this important milestone.

The great thing about seeking work when you're young is that virtually every possibility is open to you. There's nothing that you *can't* do, and little that you *won't* do. If you haven't amassed any financial or familial responsibilities, you're much freer to relocate than many others who've been in the workforce for some time. That can make you an attractive hire and open even more doors.

You may be worrying that your shortage of experience will hamper your search and limit your options, but that isn't necessarily the case. True, you may lack leverage when it comes to bargaining over wages or work conditions, but in a soft economy, your inability to command an imposing salary may actually work in your favor. It's a topsy-turvy way of thinking, but when the economy goes south, entry-level candidates can be preferable to heavy-hitting veterans. If you have the opportunity, enjoy this status and exploit it—it's unlikely to last forever.

One virtue that you must bring to your search is patience. As eager as you are to get to work, you might be tempted to snatch the first opportunity that comes along just so that you can cash that historic first paycheck. In your situation, you can afford to be more discriminating. Scrutinize each offer carefully. You're not so much concerned with compensation at this point as you are with the qualitative aspects of prospective jobs—the valuable experiences that they provide, and the paths to advancement that they spread before you.

If an offer comes up short in these key components, don't hesitate to reject it and continue your search. You have so much going for you that better opportunities are sure to materialize. The thrill of joining the labor force will be that much more intense when you select exactly the right job.

4.

Keep Your Goals in Sight

In the throes of a job search, potential distractions are plentiful. It isn't creature comforts that will seduce you; you're experienced and capable enough to realize the dangers there. However, it can be difficult when gathering so much information and moving in so many different directions at once to lose sight of your main goal.

For example, on a given day, you may review hundreds of classified ads from both print and online sources. You may fill out and submit a handful of applications, schedule several interviews, make a few follow-up calls, and garner information from friends and family about still other opportunities. Measured by volume alone, this seems a productive day, but it may not move you any closer to your objective if your goals are buried beneath this barrage of information.

What is it that you want to accomplish with your job search? It's a deceptively difficult question—not everyone answers it the same way. For some, finding a job, any job, is the most vital outcome. It's reasonable for job seekers in this situation to follow up any and every lead, no matter the type of position or the compensation package.

If your target is a senior position in your chosen field, however, then you must be disciplined enough to ignore even the most enticing opportunities outside your area of expertise. These won't get you where you want to go, so there's no sense wasting resources to pursue them. Similarly, if your goal is a second career, following up leads in your former specialty won't help you launch that next phase of your professional life. Instead, use your time to research the market for employment in your new field and explore appropriate training programs, should you deem those necessary.

Keep your goals in sight, and you won't squander precious time and money on secondary concerns. If you share your principal goals with family and friends, they might be able to help keep you on course. By asking you, "How will that help you achieve your objective?" they could restore the proper focus.

5.

Beware of Time Frames

When you're out there on the front lines searching for a job, you might be tempted to set a deadline for yourself. You look at your savings and other financial resources, and you conclude, "I have enough money to last three months, so I *must* have a job by then." Linking the length of your search to your available resources may seem pragmatic, but it also can be a formula for a serious mismatch.

Suppose that the three months to which you've limited yourself are about to expire, and you've yet to discover a winning employment match. With your self-imposed deadline looming, should you accept any offer just to have some cash coming in? Do that and you might find yourself stuck in a position that provides you with little satisfaction or one that doesn't use your talents appropriately. This is not an appealing scenario.

According to the outplacement firm Challenger, Gray & Christmas, the average job search for discharged managers and executives in the first quarter of 2002 lasted 3.4 months. Your search may be shorter or longer, depending on the type of position that you're seeking, but the job market is unlikely to be prodded along by your financial situation—however urgent.

There's also the important question of your state of mind. If you establish a deadline, you may feel increasingly anxious when that deadline approaches. This tension can contribute to a vicious cycle: Not being able to find the right position might make you irritable and uneasy, which in turn will make you a less attractive job candidate, to say nothing of a less productive family member. This is self-imposed pressure that you don't need—the task before you is tough enough.

Rather than setting deadlines, approach your search with the idea that you're not working against the clock. If your cash reserves are dwindling, explore ways of extending or enhancing them, rather than accepting an ill-advised position. Your search should take as long as it takes to find the right solution.

6.
Is Relocation in Your Future?

At some point in your search, you may wonder if it doesn't make sense for you to pack up the family and relocate. Despite your best efforts, you can't find anything in your field—at least not anything that would provide you with the financial and intellectual rewards that you need. If you worked for the major employer in your region, or for a company that served as a supplier for that large firm, you may encounter this dilemma earlier in your search rather than later. When your town's dominant employer doesn't have jobs in your specialty, chances are that smaller firms won't have those jobs, either.

Clearly, relocation is a major decision for you, but don't let it provoke needless anxiety. Weigh all the factors, just as you do at each of life's watershed moments, and you'll come up with the right answer.

Consider, for example, what might await you elsewhere. Are you guaranteed a position if you relocate, or would your search be just as speculative in another market? Think also about the cost of living in other communities. If you relocate to a town where housing and transportation costs are fifty percent higher than they are where you live now, what sort of compensation package would you need to make up the difference, and are you likely to land a position that attractive?

Personal factors should be considered, as well. How would relocation affect your children and their education? Would you be moving further from family members who might need you—just as you might need them—in a crisis?

Ask all these questions as objectively as you can. Then convene a family council, and sketch the choices for your loved ones. Their input will be vital in helping you resolve this dilemma.

Your decision here won't necessarily be immutable. Over time, as your professional and family situations change, you may find that relocation becomes more or less appealing. If you apply thoughtful and objective decision-making skills to the task, you'll come away with a choice that you and your family can embrace.

7.

Cast Your Net Wide

P romising job leads may come from anywhere, so it follows that you must cast your net wide throughout your search. Some sources may be more likely to help than others, so you'll want to spend more of your time with those sources—but don't rule anything out.

It's easy to make the mistake of focusing exclusively on the outlets of information with which you're most familiar. If you've spent your career creating and placing print advertising, for example, it would be no surprise if you concentrated on help wanted ads in your local newspaper. If you're a "New Economy," veteran, you might instead rely on web-based lead services. You'll be within your comfort zone if you adopt this strategy, but you might be missing opportunities by limiting your information pool.

A typical day of your job search should include visits—literal and figurative—with many sources. You can review newspaper classified ads with your morning coffee. Then you might repair to your computer to click on the employment web sites that you've bookmarked. Chances are that you'll still have time before lunch to touch base with friends and members of your job network to see how they're doing—and to learn if they've unearthed any leads for you.

The lunch hour may not be a good time to reach people in the office, but you can make use of this slow time by swinging by the local unemployment office and checking the bulletin boards for any appropriate openings. Think also of the newsletters of any professional or special-interest organizations to which you belong and any alumni publications that you receive. These groups may have web sites for you to explore. Of course, you won't receive these publications every day, but make it a point to check for any job opportunities as soon as they hit your mailbox.

You might not be able to check every source, every day; ideally, you'll be scheduling interviews that will occupy a big chunk of your time, and you'll have resumes to send and applications to fill out and submit, as well. When you cast your nets wide, though, you're well on the way to a successful—and early—conclusion to your search.

8.

Form Support Groups

Very few endeavors in life are as lonely as a job search. You send off resumes and very often hear nothing from the companies that you've targeted. You fill out applications and get precious little feedback from the hiring managers involved. You apply for unemployment compensation and find that the process is now consummated by phone, eliminating opportunities for face-to-face contact.

The good news, if you can call it that, is that many others are engaged in the same lonely quest as you. When you get together with people in exactly the same circumstances as you, you can conquer the sense of isolation by swapping notes, contacts, and experiences with them. You'll be amazed at how fulfilling networking with other unemployed folks can be.

It won't be hard to find members for your network. If you were caught up in a massive downsizing at your old job, there might be dozens of your former colleagues who'll be eager to trade information with you. The unemployment office is another place to build your network. Of course, this means that you'll need to visit the office rather than handle your benefits by phone, but you'll find your trips worthwhile. Conversations will flow freely—everyone already knows that finding a job is the issue, so you can cut to the chase.

When your network gathers at the local café or coffee shop, you'll have many timely topics to discuss. You can share news of job opportunities, including those that seem promising and those that turned out to be dead ends. Think of the time and energy that you'll save if your network informs you that a position you saw advertised actually will be filled internally. You can support your friends when they're down, and they'll return the favor for you.

When a member of your network lands a position, that's great news. Not only does it validate the prospects of your own search, but it means that a new friend of yours is on the inside of a company—and well-positioned to give you a heads-up on any openings.

9.

Online Can Be Fine

As you gather tools for your job search, you may wonder what role online employment sites should play. If you're new to the web and not conversant with—or confident about—its uses and features, you may well feel some ambivalence about going online to look for work. Your uncertainty is not without justification, as there are advantages and drawbacks to this particular application of the Internet.

One strong advantage is the scope of coverage that online sources can offer. If you rely on classified ads in the local newspaper, your search is basically limited to your immediate locale. Internet employment sites can alert you to opportunities across the nation—or in any region that you select. This regionalization of postings will be especially valuable if you're considering relocation. Just click on your target area, and you have a set of opportunities in your preferred area.

Immediacy is another advantage of online communication. You don't have to depend on a print shop to produce your resumes in a

31

timely fashion, and you're not at the whim of postal mail service. Once you've prepared the electronic version of your resume, you can convey it anywhere, in a matter of seconds, with a single click of your mouse. It's not inconceivable that a prospective employer could respond to your resume or application within moments of your transmitting it.

But online job sites bring a downside as well. An obvious concern is that you may not be entirely sure who's on the other end of your e-mail, an inherent problem with electronic communication. And you won't be able to drive by the facility to inspect it if it's out there in cyberspace.

The broad accessibility of the Internet also means a potential quantum leap in the number of applicants for any position. If you notice an appealing online opportunity, chances are that thousands of others will follow the same route, making the competition more intense than ever.

Thus, online employment sites are neither the answer, nor are they to be avoided. They're one resource among many that you should tap throughout your job search. It's easy enough to build a sweep of appropriate Internet sites into your daily routine—and just as easy to remember that your search must extend beyond the Internet.

10.

Online Resumes

Among the online features accessible to you, one of the most interesting possibilities is posting your resume electronically at appropriate web sites. Such postings resemble the "Situations Wanted" component of your daily newspaper's classified ads, but differ in one key regard. Instead of notifying only local companies of your availability, you're conveying your credentials to the entire online universe.

Awesome as this reach may be, there are dangers here. If your contact information is part of your resume as it ordinarily would be, you may be aggravating your vulnerability to identity theft. At the very least, posting your e-mail address could subject you to relentless e-mail solicitations from every ambitious or unscrupulous marketer in cyberspace. Thus, it's important to review the privacy policies of sites where you're posting to understand how they might distribute your address.

In fact, the employment web site Job-Hunt.org considers posting your resume without protecting your privacy as the biggest mistake online job seekers can make. One solution is to mask or suppress your contact information. Should you elect this option, prospective employers will have to jump through an electronic hoop to reach you, but you'll have the comfort of knowing your identity and privacy are more secure.

Two suggestions for online job searching:

Don't send your resume as an attachment. Many companies are so fearful of computer viruses that they no longer open attachments. If you happen to communicate with one of these firms, your attachment won't do you much good. As an alternative, paste your resume in the message box, or paste it and attach it, to give recipients a choice.

Make sure your computer is virus-free. The last thing a company needs is to lose valuable time and incur unbudgeted costs cleaning up an electronic bug. The last thing you need is to be the hapless applicant who transmits that pesky germ. If you install anti-virus software, you can be reasonably confident that no message from you will be infectious.

11.

When Headhunters Hunt *Your* Head

You may not be looking for work, but that doesn't mean you won't be solicited. This can happen when "headhunters"—recruiting specialists whom companies engage to help identify and attract talented people, most often at the executive level—get your name on their prospect lists.

Typically, headhunters will learn of you through recommendations from other prospects or clients in their fold. They may engage in some discreet research to flesh out their files on you. Even though you haven't shown the slightest restlessness in your current position, they may contact you anyway on the theory that no one will ignore an opportunity for improvement.

Their initial calls to you can be cloaked in secrecy. They don't want to leave a voice mail or send an e-mail that's too specific, lest one of your colleagues or supervisors access the message and conclude—however incorrectly—that you're in the job market. So their messages will sound something like this: "When you call me back, I'll clear up the mystery about why I'm trying to reach you."

When you finally make contact with your headhunter, you have every right to be flattered by this unsolicited attention; they wouldn't be pursuing you if your performance weren't eye-catching. But even as you're feeling good about yourself, it may be wise to proceed with caution. Headhunters' understanding of who you are usually is superficial. They're trying to fill a job opening, and they know you work generally in the right field. Beyond that, they have little sense of your talents and no inkling of your job preferences. What they have might be considered a category match, and little more.

If you do indicate an initial interest in this very preliminary inquiry, you could trigger a series of phone calls, meetings, and interviews that prove awkward and difficult to schedule around your current professional responsibilities—and all for a position you may not even desire.

Keep your goals in mind. If the position described by the headhunter is consistent with your career goals, continue the process. But if the proposed job clashes with your overall objectives, let the headhunter know that as soon as possible. That will end the recruitment and prevent any conflict with your current employer. When appropriate, you also can advise the headhunter that you might be interested in a new position down the road, and that you'd appreciate being contacted for future opportunities. It won't hurt to have that option should your circumstances change.

12.

Responding to Classified Ads

Every job seeker who's dealt with classified ads can tell you horror stories about using them to find jobs. You may respond immediately to a classified ad—the very day that it appears in the newspaper—yet you're advised that the position has been filled. This is a pretty good indication that the ad wasn't designed to solicit so much as it was a fulfillment of corporate human resources policies. You may follow up an ad that appears to promise a satisfying position in public relations, only to learn that what the employer really wants is telemarketers. There's nothing wrong with telemarketing, except that it's not the job that you thought you were pursuing.

Even an ad that appears to accurately describe a position, salary, and benefits can be troublesome if it masks the identity and location of the advertiser. If you're directed to respond to a post office box, or Department C, or Drawer F, to what type of company are you entrusting your resume? You can't really know.

Throw in the lack of feedback from most classified advertisers, and this may not seem like a fruitful vehicle for your job search. Still, you have access to thousands of job ads every day—in your local newspaper, through online placement services, and sometimes, even on a local cable television show dedicated to job matches. Many of them are legitimate and worth pursuing. In the word "classified," you'll see both "class" and "if." To avoid wasting precious time and resources, your task is to separate the "class" ads from the "iffy" ads.

Beware of blind ads. Businesses might shield their identities for a number of reasons, but if you don't know who's advertising, you can't tell if this position makes sense for you. Prioritize ads that fully describe the position and company.

If the position is high-profile and unique, exercise caution. A firm looking for a CEO or a university seeking a head basketball coach typically will use a headhunter or word of mouth rather than classified ads. They may advertise these positions, but the ads are nominal, not designed to yield anything. On the other hand, if your local cable company advertises for fifty technicians for a rebuilding project, you know that they need people in bulk. In this case, you can respond with more confidence.

Watch out for "up to's." You've seen these ads: "Earn up to $100,000 at home." Sure, somebody at that company might be earning $100,000, but you're likely to start at a much lower level.

It can be daunting weeding out the "good" ads from the "bad" ones. You'll save yourself much disappointment if you are able to discern early on the kind of advertising to which you are responding.

13.

Keep the Faith

It's not inconceivable that your job search may drag on to the point where you begin to feel despair nibbling at the edges of your calm. This is the time to keep the faith. You've been in tight spots before, and your talent, persistence, and belief in yourself always have brought you through. Remind yourself that this job search is nothing more than a blip on your bright career screen, and it will end successfully.

Keep your faith in others, as well. Your family has been with you this far. You've counted on their support, and you can continue to rely on it. In fact, if the truth be known, our families often have more faith in us than we have in ourselves—especially in times of crisis. This vote of confidence from your family should reinforce your self-confidence.

Also have faith in the system. This may be the most difficult faith of all to sustain. It's the system, after all, that's left you in this professional rut—but that same system is working now, however slowly, to bring you back on board. Even if it takes longer than you had hoped, just keep on keeping the faith.

14.

Be Your Own Matchmaker

If you engage an employment agency, it will likely walk you through some exercises designed to determine your ambitions on the one side and your aptitude and experience on the other. You might think of these drills as a skills assessment, and it's an essential tool for outsiders trying to place you. You may not have the resources to bring on such a consultant, but you're eminently qualified to prepare your own skills assessment worksheet—so long as you undertake this task objectively.

Here's the way to do it. On the left-hand side of a clean sheet of paper, jot down the occupation that you most desire—call it "Manager" for the purposes of this demonstration. Under "Manager," write the headings for two categories: "Skills" and "Experience." Now, enter under those categories the skills and experience that you think a solid managerial candidate should offer. Some examples of appropriate entries might be ability to motivate people; ability to build a team spirit among people of varied opinions and background; or experience with budget preparation and execution.

On the right-hand side of the paper, list your own skills and experience in matching sections. You're ready now to review your handiwork. If there's a general fit between your characteristics and those that the position requires, you're beginning your job search with a conceptual match that bodes well for success. If, however, you find that you fall short of the requirements in certain areas, you may be facing a choice.

You might find the gap too broad to bridge within a few weeks or months. In this scenario, it might be reasonable to set your sights on some other position. You might also find that you're tantalizingly close to where you need to be. Some skills-based training could provide you with the necessary qualifications and keep you on track for your most desired position.

When you serve as your own matchmaker, there's always the danger that your self-evaluation will be less than objective, so it's a good idea to share your assessment with friends and mentors, who are less likely to be influenced by emotion. If necessary, modify your worksheet based on their input. When your assessment is completed, you'll be ready to pursue your preferred position with confidence, because you'll know you've made a great match.

15.

Freshen Up Skills and Learn New Ones

If you lost your job in a downsizing, chances are that the action had little to do with your performance. You might have been the most capable employee ever, but if your position was targeted for elimination, not even your competence could save you. Now, though, the success of your job search will depend on your professional record and talents. It's a great time to evaluate those skills—and enhance them where necessary.

Take a critical look at your resume. Do you have the skill base that would attract a new employer? If not, where do you fall short? It's those areas that you might want to address now.

For example, how are your computer skills? You likely acquired and utilized basic skills at your former job, but much has happened in the cyber-universe since then. Get current! Take a course in desktop publishing or web design. You even could pursue a certificate in those or related disciplines. It's always impressive to include notice of certification on a resume.

Facility with computers is an obvious area for freshening, but there are many others. Does your honest self-critique tell you that your career has been slowed by inadequate public speaking skills? You can fill that need now.

Updating talents that you already have should be a key goal, as well—particularly if you worked for one employer for many years. Your company may have done things one way, yet other approaches probably have developed while your firm was married to a specific system. This is particularly true in such areas as inventory control and supply chain management, where science has progressed rapidly. Freshening skills in your areas of expertise can only help.

Once you decide to broaden your skill base, you'll find many accessible training vehicles, including online tutorials, seminars, and courses at local community colleges. There might be tuition involved, but that's a minor thing in the quest to make you the most attractive job candidate possible.

16.

An Investment in Your Future

You can view your job search in several ways. Each has consequences for the outcome of your quest and the level of tension that you feel along the way.

You may perceive your search as a desperate scramble to find an income source that will help you pay your mounting bills. Then, when you grasp for any old job, that's likely what you'll get—any old job—all but guaranteeing continued pressure and unhappiness before too long.

You can also look at your search as a piece of drudgery, a protracted chore that brings you no pleasure but must be endured for the sake of your family. Yet if you believe that circumstances have conspired to force you to seek a job, you're not likely to feel the enthusiasm that successful searches require. You may experience a growing resentment that justifies shortcuts and sloppiness, neither of which will yield the position that you want.

A better mental framework for your search is to consider it an investment in your future. No one would be callous enough to suggest that the loss of your previous job was a blessing, but that doesn't mean that good things can't arise from the wreckage. When you were working, your time and talent largely were controlled by others. Your future was in their hands, and their vision for you may not have extended beyond the next quarterly earnings report. Now, you have an opportunity to shape your own destiny, to develop the career that you've always wanted. Once you seize this opportunity, your search no longer will seem boring, forced, or pressure-packed.

Remembering your investment in your future also can help on the financial front. If you consider your job search a chore, you may be unwilling to allocate any financial resources to it, which ultimately could render your quest less productive. When you're investing in your future, you spend what it takes to prepare a great resume or sharpen your skills, because you know that you're creating a future that will repay these expenses many times over.

If you've ever invested in the stock market, you know how interested you can become in the companies that you've purchased. You follow their fortunes closely, and you exult in even the smallest gains in share prices. It's a riveting experience. Investing in your future through a job search brings the same attentiveness and excitement. Not only is it captivating, but there's also a handsome payoff awaiting you.

17.

Considering a Career Shift?

L oss of your job can propel you to seek another, but it also can be the impetus for a bold new revelation—you weren't very satisfied with your career, and you're not all that upset about leaving your old position. If you catch yourself flirting with these thoughts, don't resist them. They might be an indication that a career shift is in order.

Of course, changing professions at a relatively mature age is a dramatic action, and one not to be taken lightly. You might find it necessary to acquire new skills in a training program, or even to pursue a new degree or certificate. A career shift also might mean an extended period of modest income while you work your way up the ladder. If you and your family can handle such financial challenges, a second career can be energizing.

Launching a new career puts you in a learning mode, and there's little that's more satisfying than acquiring a new set of skills. You emerge from your training more versatile—adept in even broader ways. That's certain to boost your self-image. Moreover, you become a much more valuable commodity in the job market. Not only do you bring your new talents to any employers, but you also offer all of the abilities that you mastered in your previous career.

One of the important new features of our economy is that we tend to work longer into our lives, often beyond the traditional retirement age of sixty-five. Because senior citizens are more welcome than ever before in the workforce, you'll likely be able to practice your new profession for several decades, at least. This wrinkle makes even multiple careers a real possibility.

Begin your quest for personal diversity with a little research. If you find out what's hot in the market, you may be able to shape your occupational desires to the economy's most pressing needs. Your research also should give you a sense of where you can learn your new profession and what your training period might cost.

If your initial findings are cautionary—the learning curve is too long, the price is too high—don't be discouraged. Keep at it until you find the perfect new career track. You owe it to yourself to explore all of the possibilities.

18.

"I'm Unemployed"

To a regrettable extent, society defines us by our jobs rather than who we are as individuals. This never was the most fruitful or fair way to judge people and it makes even less sense in our modern era, when jobs tend to be ephemeral instead of lifelong pursuits. Be that as it may, you may feel diminished—in your own mind and in the way that you imagine others perceive you—if you become unemployed.

We've developed a whole glossary of euphemisms to cushion this blow to our self-esteem. We're not unemployed, we tell ourselves and others. We're between jobs. We're transitioning. We're consulting. We do not like to think of ourselves as having been "fired." We allow that we've been furloughed, laid off, severed, or downsized. The problem is not that these descriptions are untrue; one or more of them may describe your situation accurately. The real danger is that using such language may seduce you into thinking that your situation isn't as bad as all that, and that you don't really need to spring into action.

Action, though, is what's called for. If you find yourself traveling down Denial Drive, it's high time to change directions. Deny your denial. Be unemployed without shame. If you continue to use frank terminology to describe your circumstances, you're more likely to undertake an effective, timely job search.

Do you find the word "unemployed" difficult to get over? Practice it. Stand before a mirror and repeat the words "I'm unemployed" until they both feel and sound natural. Check out your body language as you repeat the sentence. Are you slumping and shying away from your own image? Then straighten up. Do you glance downward in the same way that you might avert your gaze in the presence of peers? Keep your eyes forward.

Say "I'm unemployed" in the same matter-of-fact way that you might say "I'm left-handed," or "I'm a Leo." It's a description that should imply neither pride nor shame. When you're able to adopt this matter-of-fact attitude about your unemployment, you've found the right starting point for your job search.

19.

Your Job Characteristics Checklist

Under economic and psychological pressure, you may grasp at the first job offer that comes along. This certainly will provide immediate income and temporary peace of mind, but that sense of well-being may be short-lived if the position turns out to be a poor match for your talents, expectations, and needs. If it's a gross mismatch, you could find yourself back on the job hunt, feeling even more intense pressure than you did the first time around.

There's a lot to be said for thoroughly exploring any job offer before making your decision. You might even draw up a "job characteristics checklist" to help you pursue all the vital information and subject each offer to thorough evaluation. Try these categories for your checklist.

- *Compensation*—this will be the most visible aspect of any job offer, but you'll still have some research to do. For instance, does the position offer any bonus potential, and what performance levels would trigger the bonus? Are performance reviews conducted

50

annually, semiannually, or on some other schedule? You also can determine the length of pay periods—weekly, biweekly, and monthly are typical—and whether direct deposit is an option.

- *Benefits*—often, we don't fully understand the benefits scheme until we labor through the new-hires package. You can get ahead of the curve by inquiring about medical insurance, disability and life insurance, vacations and holidays, sick days, and personal days. Ask also about stock participation and any company-sponsored retirement programs, such as 401(k) plans. Find out about wellness programs and onsite day care and senior care opportunities. Not all companies offer these, but if your prospective employer does, that can be a powerful factor in your decision.

- *Transportation*—how long will it take you to get to and from work? If the total commute is, say, two hours or more, is that how you want to spend your time? Think also about the costs. If public transportation isn't available, do you want to incur the expenses of an automobile? How about parking costs? If these would average $200 per month, that would effectively reduce the salary offer by $2,400 a year—a significant hit.

- *Style*—would you be working in a private office, a cubicle, or shared space? Are flexible times and telecommuting possibilities? No single set of job characteristics works for everybody, of course, but with a little probing, you can determine whether a job would be just your style.

51

20.

What You Bring to the Table

Job interviews can be intimidating. On one side of the table sits "the Company," a large, prosperous organization that—in your mind, anyway—will continue to thrive if it doesn't hire you. On the other side of the table sits you, whose savings and self-esteem are running dry and who needs a job in the worst way. If you perceive the interview as a one-sided mismatch, you're doing yourself a tremendous disservice. You bring a lot to this table.

For one thing, you have talent—in fact, a diversity of skills that would benefit any employer. Should you doubt it, take a fresh look at the very resume that you prepared for this interview. That should remind you of the wide range of assignments which you've handled. Throw in the capabilities that you've developed off the job, through such activities as child-rearing, volunteering, and fundraising, and you will see one multitalented job applicant.

In addition, you bring experience to the fray. Because you've worked in a group environment before, you understand how to be a team player and how to reflect and enhance the corporate culture. There's no long learning curve for you—you'll be ready to contribute in short order. High on your list of attributes should be your positive, can-do attitude. You've met countless challenges in the past, and you have confidence that you'll do so in your new position.

If you're able to take this broad view of the asset package known as you, you'll be inspired by the knowledge that you're a versatile powerhouse—skilled, experienced, industrious, and vital. You may not be able to leap tall buildings in a single bound, but you'll know how to orchestrate that leap, how to assign tasks, and how to allocate resources, should your employer ever need to jump that high.

Once you reacquaint yourself with your own talents, your confidence level will soar—and that faith and optimism will be evident to any interviewer. Hiring managers will fully appreciate what you bring to the table—your attitude will announce it, loud and clear.

21.

It's Not a One-Way Street

If your job search has been long and vexing, you may be tempted to snap up the first offer that comes your way without negotiating a better deal for yourself. Remember, you bring a unique set of skills, experience, and personality strengths to the table. In fact, you may be such an attractive package that the company will go beyond its announced salary and benefits to land you.

Veteran negotiators often advise us never to accept the first offer, since our counterparts across the table typically leave themselves a little room to bob and weave. This theory has some applicability to job negotiations. Here, the practice of bargaining can be effective—if you negotiate over the right items and time your pitch properly. It would be unwise, for example, to ask for a heftier salary before the company has expressed its interest in you. This would be a classic example of a poorly timed negotiating ploy.

There also may be some elements of an offer that are non-negotiable. If, for example, you're applying for a customer service slot that pays seven dollars per hour for entry-level positions, and nine dollars an hour for positions on the next level, it's unlikely that the company will move from those figures. If they paid you more, they might have to similarly adjust wages throughout the workforce—an untenable position for most employers.

However, you may choose to bargain over the company's proposed grading of you. If they see you as an entry-level candidate, you might point out all of the helpful experience in your record that should qualify you as a higher-level employee from the start. This is a good example of an appropriate area for negotiation.

Once an employer has offered you a position or indicates that it intends to do so, the stage is set for even broader negotiations. Think here about salary and benefits, such as vacation time. The employer may advise you that new hires aren't eligible for vacation for the first six months. You, on the other hand, might need a few days to attend a family reunion or take a trip already planned, so it's reasonable to bargain for that vacation time.

After you reach conceptual agreement with your prospective employer, the specifics of your hiring can be a product of give and take. Most firms will think more of you rather than less if you attempt to negotiate a few items; it suggests your confidence in your abilities. The key to successful negotiations is understanding what to ask for—and when.

22.

Don't Be Seduced by Salary

No question about it, salary is big. It can determine how much money you have to spend and, just as vital, how much you're able to save. A generous salary also can contribute to a healthy self-image; the value of that never should be underestimated. So when you're pursuing your next position, it's natural to prioritize salary over other characteristics of the prospective job.

However, a hefty salary can be sweetly, falsely seductive. Consider this situation. You're offered a position with an annual salary of $40,000 but no bonus potential. As you're pondering that, you receive another job offer. This one would pay you $35,000, but you could earn a bonus up to twenty percent, which translates to $7,000. With the first job and its bigger salary, you're guaranteed $40,000 but no more. With the second position and its seemingly less attractive salary, you have the opportunity to earn $42,000.

Which is the better offer? The answer isn't clear, since you would want to weigh the criteria for bonus eligibility, among other things. What is clear is that the position with the richer salary isn't necessarily the better option for you.

Think also of all the other factors that play a role in job satisfaction, such as length of commute, work environment and culture, and the stability of the employer. That $40,000-per-year job sounds great, but it might not be quite so attractive if it involves a total daily commute of three hours. If you could reclaim them, those fifteen hours each week that you spend fighting traffic might be more valuable to you than the most lucrative salary.

Similarly, if you're accustomed to having your own office, what sort of salary tradeoff would it take to make you happy working in a cubicle or bullpen environment? If you sign on for a high-paying job with a shaky company that might experience layoffs not too far down the road, what have you gained, and what have you lost?

Instead of evaluating jobs on salary only, it may be more productive to consider the entire compensation and work environment package. If you've developed your goals in these areas, you'll know exactly the job characteristics you want, and you won't be seduced by salary.

23.

Understanding the Whole Deal

The relationship between a company and its personnel used to be a whole lot simpler. Employees provided their labor, received a paycheck, and looked forward to two weeks of vacation, and that was as complicated as the deal got. The advent of benefits changed the simplicity of this equation forever. Benefits packages have become so varied and multifaceted that it's difficult to evaluate job offers until you know the particulars of the benefits programs involved.

Many companies, for example, offer their employees coverage through a health maintenance organization (HMO), which may provide the full measure of reimbursement only if you use medical professionals who participate in the plan—"in-network coverage" is the common term for it. Go outside the network and you pay more. Whether or not your providers are in-network could be an important factor in your consideration of a position, yet that information might not be available to you at the interview stage.

Pension plans are another aspect of the benefits package that could be extremely important, particularly if you view your company pension as your most important savings vehicle. Pension plans are complicated and can raise a series of questions: Does the company make a contribution, and if so, is it tied to your contribution? Who manages the plan, and is there a fee for that? Do you have the flexibility to add assets that you select, or are you limited to company stock? Are your earnings taxable? Tax-free? Tax-deferred? Clearly, these are elements of the plan that you need to know. Pose these questions in your interview, however, and you'll likely receive nothing more than a quizzical look.

The key to understanding the whole deal may be appropriate timing of your request for information. If you ask too early in the process, it may seem you're assuming that an offer is forthcoming—a show of self-assuredness that may come off negatively to a hiring manager. However, once an employer has expressed formal interest in you, the hiring manager will understand that you need to familiarize yourself with every detail of the benefits package and will be eager to provide the materials that you need. After all, it's in the employer's interest, as well, that your decision be informed. Unpleasant surprises could make for unhappy employees—something that no company wants.

24.

Is Diversity More Than Cursory?

Your job search may seem tough today, but imagine what it might have been like perhaps fifty years ago, when many employers discriminated against minorities—more or less actively. If members of minorities lost their jobs, there was real cause for alarm; finding new positions in an economy stacked against them was just about hopeless.

It would be naïve to assume that discrimination has disappeared and that the employment playing field has been leveled so that all have an equal chance. However, thanks to changes in attitude and the inspiration offered by a number of progressive laws, employers of all sizes today have diversified their workplaces. The challenge, of course, is finding those companies.

No employer ever will admit to anything less than a full-fledged commitment to diversity, but we know that some will exaggerate their record on this score. Where a prospective employer is concerned, how can you be sure that diversity is more than cursory?

Some human resources (HR) experts recommend that at some point in the hiring process, you tour the employer's facilities to get a sense of the company's population. This can be helpful in some ways. If an employer suggests that it has equipment that enables those with disabilities to execute all jobs, your site inspection can help verify that. Just remember that your tour is showing you a slice of the workforce that may not be representative and can be superficial or misleading. Seeing other minorities on the shop floor may cheer you, but that tells you little about the career development paths open to minorities.

You also may use your interview to probe the state of diversity, but your questions must be specific and to the point. If you ask, "Do you practice diversity in hiring and promoting?" you can be pretty sure of getting the party line in reply. If your question is more targeted—something like, "Do you have any programs to help veterans make the transition to civilian life?"—you eliminate the wiggle room.

Solicit members of your job network for any diversity information that they might have about your potential employer. Talk to as many current and former workers as you can, and research this as thoroughly as possible. The strength of an employer's commitment to diversity can be its defining characteristic.

25.

The Perfect Match

I deally, your job search will yield the perfect match. You'll find the job that provides a comfortable and fair compensation package, a productive working environment, and plenty of opportunity for both creative challenge and advancement. Your office will be but a quick bus ride or car trip from your home, and you'll make many fast friends among your new colleagues.

From your employer's point of view, the fit will be perfect, as well. The company will benefit from an experienced, talented worker who's ready to step in and contribute immediately, without a lengthy learning curve.

If your job search threatens to bog down and this dream job seems just that—a dream—keep pressing forward. You *will* find it, or a position very close to it. Should you doubt it, consider the case of Laura, who had developed considerable skills in call-center supervision over the first decade of her career. When her employer downsized, Laura was left without work—and without immediate prospects—despite her outstanding resume.

For the next ten nerve-wracking months, there was little change. Laura had a few nibbles, but the opportunities seemed far less than perfect to her, and she didn't follow up. She accepted the lifestyle sacrifices of her extended search, keeping the faith that something better was in the offing. She was right. Eleven months after losing her job, she was offered a position as a call-center manager. The salary was no more than comparable to her previous pay, but the professional challenges excited her.

If you can afford the wait and the sacrifices, it will be worth it for you, as well. The perfect professional match for you is out there. When you find it, the temporary hardships that you endured will seem insignificant against the satisfactions of your new role.

26.

Settling for Less

The goal of your job search is the consummate position for you—work that provides handsomely for you and your family while offering you a fertile environment for creativity and satisfaction. There's every reason to believe that you'll achieve your objective, if only you can allow enough time for the process.

Alas, if the time frame of your job search is compressed by compelling financial needs, you may feel pressure to settle for something less—even to snap up the first concrete offer that comes along. Unappetizing as this situation may be, it's hardly uncommon. Most of us at one time or another have accepted work that really didn't inspire us, assuring ourselves that it was only for a little while. Once we paid off our bills, we would move on to bigger and better things.

However, settling for less—in the hope that you'll find more later—can be a trap. It's much more challenging to look for work when you're already working. Your time now is committed to your employer; you'll be forced to slip away during lunch or after hours to pursue leads. Inevitably, the job search that you've now resumed becomes less than comprehensive.

Remember, the perfect job is elusive—that's why you had to settle for less in the first place. If you're able to devote less energy to the search because you're employed full time, the chances of finding that breakout position become even more remote. When you think of your colleagues and former colleagues, it's easy to identify the ones who settled for less. They're the people who were constantly on edge and usually complaining about something.

That's not the route for you. Rather than settling for less, do everything that you can to extend the time and resources which you can dedicate to your job search. If credit card debt is the chief culprit, try consolidating your debts to reduce your monthly bill— and the pressure to accept any old offer. If your parents and other family members have offered their help, now may be the time to accept it. They'll be delighted if their assistance helps you land that dream job. For your sake and theirs, get creative, hunker down, and hold out for as long as you can.

27.

If You've Been Shown the Door

When you lose your job, it can be the loneliest feeling in the world. That door closes for the last time, and you fear that it's shutting you out of the rich tapestry of satisfactions, achievements, and memories that highlighted your tenure. You may worry that you're walking this path alone, but an astounding number of people are on the same road.

In 1996, according to the Bureau of Labor Statistics (BLS) of the U.S. Department of Labor, 1,437,628 American workers were first-time applicants for unemployment insurance benefits due to mass layoffs—those where the employer projected at least fifty such claims over a five-week period. That's a horror story right there. However, by 2001, the employment picture was even worse, as the corresponding figure soared to 2,514,862—an increase of nearly 75 percent. Even these statistics understate the sweeping impact of downsizing, as they don't include workers dismissed in smaller-scale actions, and they can't account for layoff victims who don't apply for benefits or find other jobs quickly.

We never want to celebrate the misery of others, so it might be a stretch to think of others in the same boat as comforting—yet it is interesting, to say the least, that so many others are sharing your experience. This tells you two important things about your situation.

First, if you were victimized by a mass layoff, it's unlikely that your performance triggered the event. It's preposterous to imagine that more than 2.5 million workers were axed in a single year because of individual shortcomings. A sagging economy or disappointing earnings is a more plausible culprit.

Beyond that, the sheer volume of mass layoffs should indicate that an upturn is in the offing. The nation's leading businesses simply can't achieve their objectives with this huge talent pool on the sidelines. They'll need to tap it, and soon. Indeed, BLS projections support this notion, as well—the agency expects total employment to increase by fifteen percent in the decade ending in 2010. That might appear modest, but it compares favorably with the seventeen percent growth in the prosperous 1990s.

All this bodes well for your future. Soon, you'll be shown the door again—only this time, you'll be ushered into a new and rewarding phase of your career.

28.

Your Severance Package

The shock of job loss can be so severe that it may overwhelm the practical considerations that should rate a high priority. If you've lost your job—for any reason—you're probably experiencing that sense of isolation, that feeling of being adrift on a hostile sea. It's a common reaction. Your sense of self-worth, an important component of your personality, is under siege.

As understandable as this response may be, it's necessary to work through it as quickly as possible and turn to more pragmatic items— your severance package, for example. If you didn't work in the upper echelon of management, you may not think that this applies to you. You had no "golden parachute" clause, and you're not entitled to any severance pay beyond the customary two weeks' notice.

Still, there are items here that require your careful attention. Typically, a human relations specialist will review the package with you. It may include pay for such items as unused vacation time, as well as unused sick and personal days. If you were eligible for a personal performance bonus or a company performance bonus, you may be entitled to a prorated portion of your bonus. If you have outstanding expense reimbursement requests, these should be part of the severance package, too.

Even if your mood is somber and introspective at this point, these are matters that require your immediate attention. Take a close look at what the HR representative says is the cash equivalent of unused vacation time and sick and personal days. Does the company's reckoning match your records? If not, now is the time to say so. If you were eligible for a bonus and the HR professional doesn't mention it, make sure to ask. This is a typical area of neglect—not from malice, necessarily, but because employers don't usually think about your bonus eligibility once you're gone.

When you focus on your severance package, you'll be accomplishing two important goals. First, of course, you'll be maximizing the cash that will be so important to you once you undertake your job search. Just as significantly, you'll be reinforcing your own self-image as a competent person who establishes goals—and achieves them.

29.

Don't Forget Insurance

I f you're on the short end of company downsizing, you become aware of just how deeply entwined your employer was with your life. Nowhere is this more evident than in the area of insurance coverage. Most employers provide basic medical insurance, and some also offer life insurance and disability insurance.

Insurance coverage might not seem like your highest priority when you lose your job. Emotional and self-esteem issues might take precedence—but insurance shouldn't be far behind. The first step in filling any coverage gaps may be discussing your employer-provided coverage with the HR representative in your exit interview. If that seems inappropriate for any reason, you can dig out your employee manuals and a recent pay stub to determine what coverage you've been funding and what packages your employer has been providing. Now you're ready to prepare an insurance checklist, which should include these items:

Medical insurance—this, of course, is your most pressing insurance need. If your spouse participates in a plan that could include you,

review the costs and benefits of that plan. Enrollment may be a painless matter that can resolve this situation quickly and effectively, but if you lack this option, you can consider coverage through the Continuation of Benefits Recovery Act (COBRA). Through this act of Congress, you're entitled to receive the same benefits as your company provided for up to eighteen months, although your financial contribution also must continue. If nothing else, COBRA gives you some breathing space; you have the time to consider other options even as your coverage remains in place.

Life insurance—most employer-provided life insurance fails to adequately cover a family's needs, but if you never supplemented that coverage, it may be all that you ever had. You have an excellent opportunity now to review your immediate and long-range needs and map out the life insurance program that will help meet those needs.

Disability insurance—as with life insurance, the coverage that you received through your employer likely would not have equaled your financial needs in the event of disability, but it was free, and it was better than nothing. Now, you may be wondering if you can avoid disability insurance, given the other pressing financial needs that you'll encounter during your job search. Forgoing disability insurance is a roll of the dice. You're gambling on continued good health, and we all know how tenuous good health can be. At the very least, shop around for the best disability rates and coverage, so that you'll be making an informed choice.

30.

Relieving Your Pension Tension

When you lose your job, you may rue the things that you're leaving behind. Focus instead on the assets that will propel you along the next phase of your career, such as the skills that you've developed and honed, your network of professional contacts, and those colleagues who will remain your good friends no matter where you or they work next.

Another aspect of your former job that should accompany you is any pension plan that you may have been funding through your employer. In most cases, your old employer won't continue your enrollment in its retirement program, although there are some plans that will allow that. It's likely, though, that you'll need to consider other options.

One choice is to take a distribution, in effect converting this asset to cash and effectively closing out your plan. If you're facing a cash crunch, this seems like an attractive option, but it may be fool's gold. For one thing, you could face a penalty for the early distribution; that

might be a taxable event, as well. For another, you may be eliminating your principal savings vehicle—something that you always should be loath to do.

Another option is to roll over your account to the pension plan of your new employer. You'll avoid penalties and taxes in this scenario, which can succeed if you land another position immediately. Clearly, it won't be possible if you're facing a lengthy job search.

Yet a third choice is to roll over your balance to an individual retirement account (IRA) that you control. Of course, you'll lose any contributions and management services that your former employer provided while you were invested in the company plan. In fact, certain types of rollover IRAs prohibit additional contributions from any source—including you. However, there's a strong upside to managing your own IRA. *You* select the investments within your IRA without having to accept the sometimes limited choices offered by an employer. *You* decide when to reallocate the asset mix, and *you* determine your own distribution schedule.

You have an opportunity now to assert greater control over your own financial future. That security will go a long way to relieving any pension tension.

31.

The Credit Card Crunch

If your finances get tight during your job search, you may find yourself reaching for your credit card for both everyday and extraordinary expenses. This may help you out of a jam now, but you'll pay a steep price down the road when those charges begin to hit. Without the work-related income that you've come to count on, you may be unable to pay off your new credit card debt all at once and incur high interest rates on the balance.

Before long, you *will* land a promising new position, but do you want those first few months on your new job to be captive to the credit card charges that you ran up during your job search? That's not the happiest way to begin a new chapter in your career, and it could serve to darken your attitude about your new situation.

A better idea may be to keep those credit cards in your wallet, except for essential purchases. Plastic can be fantastic, but not in your current circumstances. Some financial advisors might counsel a more radical approach—cut up your credit cards so that you won't be tempted to use them at all—but that would leave you without credit as a valuable last resort. Besides, you've proven yourself an effective manager many times in the past; there's no doubt that you can manage your credit cards sensibly.

Part of your task here will be to fully understand the terms and conditions of your credit cards. What interest rate does each charge? If you have one card charging you eighteen percent and another charging ten percent, choosing which card to use for extraordinary expenses will be pretty easy. Minimum required payment also could come into play. Some card issuers require a minimum monthly payment of 1.5 percent; others insist that you pay at least three percent of your debt each month. Be sure to familiarize yourself with these conditions.

Search for introductory offers—no interest for six months is an example—that card issuers regularly promote. If you use such a card or transfer all your balances to that card, chances are good that when you secure your new position, you'll be able to erase your debt before any interest charges hit.

Finally, make sure that your spouse follows the same careful program—your kids, too, if they have plastic. If the entire family is exercising the same caution, you're much more likely to avoid the credit card crunch later on.

32.

Your Household Budget

Because of the pressures that they bring, job searches seem endless, yet for many people, they're relatively brief, lasting no more than a matter of weeks or perhaps a few months. When viewed against the entirety of your career, the time involved may not be significant, but when viewed against your available finances, those few weeks or months can be wrenching indeed.

Understanding your financial situation during your job search is key to keeping stress on you and your family to a minimum. If you know that your finances are secure for the next few months, you're likely to develop a strong, positive outlook about your prospects. If you're fretting over money, however, that concern could well spill over into your search itself—an attitude-killer that you definitely don't want.

The first step in getting a handle on your finances is understanding your needs and resources. If you don't typically use a household budget, now is a great time to create one. Begin with the revenue side. You no longer have salary from your former job, of course, but you may have cash from a severance package that will be a source of revenue. Factor in any income from part-time work and unemployment compensation, your spouse's paycheck, and any investment income that you may have.

Now go to the expense side of the budget, and total your typical monthly expenses. It's not always easy to remember every bill that you pay, but if you usually remit by check, your checkbook will be an excellent record for you. Don't forget those periodic costs that occur less than monthly. Some items in this category might be life insurance and auto insurance premiums, real estate taxes, and out-of-pocket medical expenses.

When you've finished itemizing, you'll have a pretty clear picture of your current financial situation, and you'll know if there's any gap between what you need and what you have. Bridging that gap will be your next step. You may not want to tap your savings, as that could adversely affect your ability to achieve your long-term goals. If you can't generate more revenue, the other option is to cut back your spending.

No single answer will fit every situation, but if you arm yourself with comprehensive information, you'll make the best decision for you and your family. In the process, you'll prevent one of the major headaches of job searches.

77

33.

Cutting Back as a Family

If you face the choice between reducing expenses and employing savings and credit cards to meet your needs during your job search, you might well opt for cutting back. It may mean a little belt-tightening now, but your savings will be available for all of your major goals, and you won't incur burdensome credit card debt in the future.

Once you develop a budget, you'll be familiar with your typical monthly expenses and the cash that is available to meet those expenses. If there's a shortfall, you are aware of where it is. That's a great starting point for a family project. Call your troops together. Let them review the figures. Explain the mission to them, and solicit their ideas on reducing expenses.

Turning budget-trimming into a family exercise serves several important purposes. First, you're liable to get some helpful ideas that you might not have considered. In the process, you'll learn which expenses your loved ones consider vital and which they regard as discretionary or even excessive. Their thoughts on what and where to cut back might differ markedly from your own.

Just as important, when you involve your family in budget-trimming, you're involving them in your job search, as well. You're reminding them that together, they constitute the most meaningful aspect of your life—more meaningful even than your career. They may not express it in so many words, but they'll be flattered and proud that you've shown confidence in them and draw closer to you and each other. In this way, something as difficult as cutting back can strengthen your family unit.

As you go through this exercise, consider some items in your budget sacred. Food, clothing, and shelter aren't necessarily such items. For example, each of you can determine to carry rather than purchase lunch; you'll get your nourishment but save money in the process.

Costs related to your job search *are* sacred. For example, if you need a car to travel to job interviews, then all expenses related to local travel—gasoline, maintenance, insurance, highway tolls—should be untouchable. No grumbling about these expenses—you're investing in your future and the happiness and security of your family. Those costs always are justified.

34.

Keep the Lines of Communication Open

While some dismissals are related to individual performance, it is more common in our current environment that a workforce reduction is triggered by poor company performance. When the economy is sluggish, many businesses fall short of their revenue and profit projections and find that they must reduce staff, since payroll is the biggest chunk of any corporate budget. In other cases, companies miscalculate a trend and find themselves in deep trouble. More often than not, the result is downsizing.

If you've been victimized by a wholesale staff cutback, you know very well that your performance wasn't to blame, yet you still might be disposed to take the action personally and vow never to have anything to do with your former employer again. Visions of sweet revenge—you'll cut them from a suppliers' list if you ever get the chance—might even dance in your head.

All dismissals include a personal element. After all, it's not a figure on a spread sheet that's been downsized; it's you, real flesh and blood. Acknowledge this, but then move beyond it. Remember that you weren't targeted in this job action, and that there may be strong advantages to maintaining cordial ties with the employer who just sent you packing.

For one thing, your former employer might provide you with a letter of reference. That could be a vital document, explaining the circumstances of your departure with more credibility than you could as a party with a vested interest. In addition, your former employer can be a source of part-time work for you as you conduct your job search. When companies downsize to save money, they soon realize that they've left themselves without adequate human resources to get the job done. They may well turn to you first for part-time or consulting projects, since they're familiar with your capabilities and outstanding work ethic. They will, if you've left the door open to such collaboration, that is.

If you lose your job, you may feel dispirited and isolated. You're entitled. Allow yourself a few days to overcome those feelings, and then make contact with your former colleagues and supervisors. It may seem ironic, but the best resource in finding a new employer can be your old employer.

35.

Unemployment Compensation

Many people find that they can absorb and adjust to the initial emotional and psychological blows of unemployment. Perhaps they moderate the impact a bit with standard corporate euphemisms. Their employers tell them that they've been downsized, severed, furloughed—anything but fired—and they, in turn, adopt this language and the slightly softer picture that it sketches. It's only when they must consider enrolling for unemployment compensation that the full weight of job loss hits them. Unemployment compensation evokes negative images for many. For them, it's a real, unavoidable indication that they've hit bottom, that they need government help to support themselves and their families, and that they're now certifiably and undeniably needy.

If this mirrors your thinking, it's high time for a major attitude adjustment. If you need resources beyond your personal income and savings to help finance your job search and daily needs, you have a strong practical motive for welcoming these benefits.

There are other reasons why the stigma attached to unemployment compensation represents an outmoded way of thinking. First, this won't be the first time that you've accepted government aid. You may not view any tax breaks that you've enjoyed in the same way that you consider unemployment compensation, but they're conceptually similar. Whether it's credits for childcare expenses, business costs, or charitable donations, the government is providing you assistance for goals that it deems important to our society. Keeping you going during your job search is no less important than those other missions, so it's natural for the government to offer help. It should be just as natural for you to accept that help.

Moreover, unemployment benefits are available only to those who qualify for them. You can't simply walk in off the street and claim this compensation. You get it only when you've enhanced the economy by working for a set period of time. In short, unemployment compensation isn't given; it's earned. Through your diligence, you've earned the right to this assistance. If it's a symbol at all, it stands for the valuable contributions that you've made throughout your career.

36.

How About Entrepreneurship?

Displaced from their jobs, more and more people have been starting their own businesses rather than face the uncertainties and frustrations of a job search. According to the U.S. Census Bureau, more than 16.5 million businesses in 2002 had no paid employees, meaning that they were most likely sole proprietorships or partnerships. These enterprises produced more than $709 billion in revenue—well beyond the $586 billion generated in 1997. The figures are impressive, but what they don't tell us is how many of these fledgling businesses will fail, or how many have faltered already, perhaps leaving the entrepreneurs worse off than they were before.

Entrepreneurship can be great. You work as your own boss in a job that you define in a business with unlimited upside. However, before trying entrepreneurship, you may want to ask some key questions about your prospects.

First, what's the market like for the products or services that you intend to provide? You may be interested in offering consulting services in marketing, but if that field already is glutted locally, will you be able to carve out a niche? You must perform your due diligence and fully research the market.

Next, can you afford the startup and operating costs? These include expenses for maintaining an office and staff, developing a product or service, and marketing your wares—all before you realize a penny in revenue. You may not want to use your own resources on such a risky enterprise, so that means soliciting bank financing or investors. You'll need the appropriate contacts and skills for that.

Finally, do you have the personal attributes that entrepreneurship requires? Dr. Tom Emerson, director of the Donald H. Jones Center for Entrepreneurship at Carnegie Mellon University, describes those characteristics this way: "They [entrepreneurs] need to learn rapidly, adapt to a changing world, and drive their vision into that world. Entrepreneurship requires a lot of creativity, an awful lot of dedication and a really agile mind."

Jack Roseman, a veteran entrepreneur who launched the Roseman Institute to mentor startup businesses, considers a passion for success—in the absence of institutional support—the most vital entrepreneurial attribute. "If you don't have that passion," Roseman says, "it ain't goin'. It's the *sine qua non*. You have to want it with all your gut. Otherwise, you'll walk away when it really gets tough."

If you want it with all your gut, then entrepreneurship may be for you—go for it. If not, don't hesitate to walk away from entrepreneurship and implement an effective job search. That will be the best choice for you.

37.

Are You a Franchise Player?

If you follow classified ads closely as part of your search, you'll notice that a disproportionate number of them appear to be opportunities to start your own business. Research a little further, and you'll find that many of these business opportunities are with franchises.

When you're a franchisee, you purchase the right to use the name of a company that's usually well established and operate your business using the franchiser's trade name. Other benefits may come along with your franchise, such as the positive impact of the franchiser's advertising, managerial assistance, and centralized purchases that may feature attractive discounts.

Franchising has an enormous but often little-known impact in most communities. You may be aware that many of the local fast-food emporiums are franchises, but the supermarkets, photocopying establishments, and automotive shops may be franchises, as well. The most successful franchisees often don't stop with a single outlet; they may own a cluster of them regionally, providing them with their own advertising and bulk purchasing muscle.

If you're considering entrepreneurship, franchising can be an attractive option, but take care. Franchise agreements often are complex. Beyond the up-front fee, you need to know who's responsible for identifying and purchasing (or leasing) the real estate where your business will be located. You'll also need to determine if you'll be allocated a percentage of the franchiser's advertising and other group costs. Are you required to purchase your equipment and supplies from the franchiser? If so, what will those costs be? Buy-back provisions, which many franchisers demand, are another area for scrutiny. Details to look for here include the conditions that would trigger a buy-back and what price you would get for your business if the franchise is reclaimed.

Franchising takes the usual complications of owning a business and ratchets them up a notch. You'll probably want some help from an attorney or a veteran franchisee in reviewing any proposed franchise agreement.

Think also of preparing a business plan before you sign on the dotted line. If you expect to seek outside financing for your franchise, most lenders would require submission of such a blueprint. Your business plan also will help you determine if you're prepared to be a franchise player.

38.

Celebrate the Success of Others

It's bound to happen—before too long, someone in your job network will land a position. While you join in the congratulations, you feel that stab of jealousy.

You hardly would be human if you didn't experience a twinge of jealousy over a friend's success, particularly when you've both been pursuing the same objective. So allow it to happen, and don't be afraid to acknowledge it or confide it to your friend.

You may catch yourself wondering, "What does my friend have going that I don't? Why has my friend's job search ended while mine plods on?" It's a great time to get beyond that feeling of envy and probe exactly those questions.

As you're enjoying a celebratory moment with your newly employed friend, pose these same questions. You may receive some valuable pointers that will invigorate your search—or you may find that you're covering much the same territory as your friend did. That will be a tremendous source of encouragement, reinforcing your determination and telling you that success is in the offing.

39.

Your Friends as Sounding Boards

You may be formally unemployed, but searching for a job usually turns out to be full-time work. Once you factor in the time that you spend combing your employment sources for opportunities, responding to ads, mailing or e-mailing resumes, filling out applications, and traveling to interviews, you have a work week that could involve more pressure and responsibility than your previous employer demanded of you.

When you went through intense, deadline-packed periods at your former job, you always could count on colleagues to ease some of the burden and see you through. You, of course, offered the same support to them. Those colleagues aren't with you now, so you need to recreate that community. Your friends can serve in this vital role.

Plan some time with friends. It can be in scheduled sessions, such as lunch or dinner with a group of buddies, a backyard barbecue that you host, or you may prefer a more relaxed affair, such as a gab session while your good pal mows the lawn. Whether these get-togethers are tightly or loosely structured, take the opportunity to use your friends as sounding boards. Your mind is cluttered with the details of your job search. Your friends aren't intimately involved with your search, so they'll be able to view developments with fresh eyes and a clear head—and they have your best interests at heart.

If you're thinking about taking your job search in a different direction, bounce the plan off your friends. Not only will they offer advice on the matter at hand, but your questions also could trigger a brainstorming binge that could lead to exciting new ideas.

Even if you hang out with the Mensa crowd, your friends won't have all the answers, but they might help steer you from extreme actions and, at the very least, give you a chance to vent some steam. If your friends offer no more than fellowship and a sympathetic ear, sometimes that's enough.

40.

Touch Base with Your Mentors

We all like to think of ourselves as self-made, but if you're truly honest about your life and career, you'll acknowledge that you've benefited from valuable advice and support along the way. Your parents, of course, may have been your earliest mentors; because they're so close to you, you may not have recognized the impact of their guidance when they offered it.

Think back to all of the others who helped steer you along the right path. Your favorite teachers not only imparted specific information, but they also helped you develop your creative processes. You may have studied with professors who led you to an understanding of the full range of your personality and capabilities. Perhaps you worked with coaches who assisted you with technique—and with some of life's tough decisions.

On the job, you had mentors, as well, even if their counseling occurred outside of any formal program. They helped you absorb the company culture, advised you of opportunities, and warned you about lurking dangers.

Guidance counselors, clergy, grandparents, and other relatives—all may have served as mentors during key periods of your life. Your job search is another of those defining times, so why not touch base with the mentors who have served you so well in the past?

Schedule friendly outings or lunches with your old mentors; you can bet that they'll be delighted to catch up with you. You'll enjoy this welcome bit of socializing that will provide some relief from the rigors of your search. Perhaps more importantly, you can solicit advice from people who want only the best for you. They're unlikely to produce specific job leads, although that certainly could happen, but they can restore your perspective, which often is the first casualty of a job search. They care about you without being intimately involved with your quest, so they can offer advice that is at once heartfelt and dispassionate. You won't stop worrying about the details, of course, but your trusted mentors can provide you with a clear view of the big picture.

41.

You'll Get Plenty of Advice

A s you conduct your job search, one thing that you won't want for is advice. Friends, family, colleagues, casual acquaintances, the mail carrier—everybody, it seems, will have a good tip on a job opportunity and how to approach it. The advice will cover the range from resume preparation to interview attire. Often, the advice will be inconsistent, even when it comes from professional sources.

For example, if you check out employment services and recruiters online, some will counsel that you need to make your resume stand out—by printing it on bright or colored paper, say—so that hiring managers will notice it. Others will contradict this strategy, suggesting that HR professionals resent nothing so much as applicants trying to lure them with cheap tricks. Some experts will advise you to ask many questions during interviews; your inquisitiveness will let hiring managers know that you're alert and committed. Still others insist that "interviewing the interviewer" is quite the wrong approach, since it may indicate to the company that you prioritize your own needs above those of the team.

All this advice can aggravate the pressure that you're feeling, perhaps confuse you, or lead you to an ill-advised course of action. Keep cool, and stick to your plan. Some advice is applicable to some situations; no advice works for all situations. What clicked for someone else may not be effective for you if your circumstances are substantially different.

Consider also the source of advice. Did you get a casual, offhand suggestion from someone that you barely know? Perhaps that's advice that can be ignored. Is it thoughtful advice from someone close to you, someone who would rejoice in your success? This may be the type of counsel to review carefully.

Glean what you can from advice, and then press forward. Even if you find that most advice isn't terribly useful, isn't it comforting to know that so many people care enough about you to offer their help?

42.

The Other Side of the Table

Among the most vexing frustrations of your job search is how impersonal it can be. At one level, you know that large companies can't take the time to respond personally to all job applicants, and you realize that it wouldn't necessarily be a wise allocation of resources to do so. At a more personal level, you've probably found yourself thinking, "If I'm ever in charge of hiring people, I'll treat applicants with more courtesy and respect."

The chances are excellent that you will eventually have the chance to implement your philosophy. You *will* find exactly the right job, you *will* become a department head, and your department *will* be in a hiring mode. What an opportunity that will be for you to inspire a kinder, gentler approach to hiring! You'll respond by mail or phone to each person who sends a resume or application, advising all of what you perceive as their strengths and shortcomings and whether or not there are openings for them.

When you interview candidates, you'll share with them the ins and outs of the hiring process so that they can work additional interviews and meetings into their schedules. You'll engage in dialogue with them, responding fully to their questions and probing for areas for a mutual fit. When you can't hire someone whom you've interviewed, you'll contact that applicant personally and explain in detail why things couldn't work out.

You'll do all this because you've been there. You've walked a mile in their shoes, and you remember that your feet hurt then as much as theirs do now. In this way, your job search can make you more empathetic—an entirely unexpected benefit, perhaps, but a benefit nonetheless.

In fact, why not let your newfound empathy inform all your dealings? There's no reason to wait until you're on the business side of the hiring table to take advantage of your broadened perspective. Your search has led you to valuable new insights. Use them now.

43.

Do Your Homework

The work of finding work may seem heavily stacked in favor of employers. They hold the jobs, they decide who will be interviewed and called back, and they control the offers and terms. It may appear that your role is limited to finding ads, responding to them, and showing up for interviews—but you can help regain a bit of the advantage by doing your homework.

Preparation can help you determine which companies to target. When you identify an opportunity, you can search online to review the web site of the company involved. While you won't learn everything that there is to know in a publicly available source, you'll discover enough about the firm to tell you whether an application from you makes sense.

Tap into your job search network, as well. You may find friends who have experience with the companies involved. Their recommendations might not be the most vital factor in your decision to pursue or not, but you'll at least come away with a better understanding of prospective new employers—and you might come away with the name of a key contact inside the company who can help even more.

Doing your homework also can prepare you for interviews. As you research companies, you'll likely come away with a few questions about their operations. When you pose these questions during interviews, you're sure to impress hiring managers with your knowledge and work ethic.

Once you commit to a full level of preparedness, you can apply that approach to still other aspects of your search. For example, imagine that you've scheduled an interview with a company in a nearby town, but you're not quite sure how to get there. Why not take a dry run over there to ensure that you won't get lost—and show up late—when it counts? Think how much more confident you'll be when you hit the road for the actual interview.

44.

News You Can Use

Here's a novel way to assure that your job search leads to the right target—read the newspaper, and pay attention to radio and TV news broadcasts. It's unlikely that you'll come up with specific leads by monitoring the news, but you will gather some information that could be helpful and save time.

Some of this good news, so to speak, may be related to conditions in certain sectors of the economy. For example, you may pick up a brief report that manufacturing throughout the country enjoyed a strong quarter. Ordinarily, you might pay token attention to this type of dispatch, but now that you're on the prowl for work, this can be a key piece of data, an indication that manufacturers soon will ramp up. If a career in manufacturing interests you, and you boast the appropriate credentials, you might want to redirect the focus of your search to this sector.

Negative news can be significant, as well. You might learn that top management at a company which you've considered approaching is under investigation for financial irregularities. Nobody has been indicted or convicted on any charges just yet, and it's possible that no one ever will be—yet you know that this firm is facing some challenging times in the short term, and it might not make the most secure landing spot for you.

Valuable as keeping up with current events can be, you don't want to be unduly influenced by news reports. Spotting trends is a tricky business; things can change quickly. Moreover, even if you accurately project a trend, that doesn't necessarily tell you anything significant about individual companies. Had you been searching for work when the dot-com bubble burst, to cite one illustration, you might have been tempted to scratch all web-based businesses off your target list—yet many dot-com companies not only survived the slump, but they're prospering to this day.

It's important to temper trend-type news reports with your research about prospective employers, their strengths, and the possibilities. If you are careful about gaining this information, chances are that you'll get good news soon.

45.

Get a Feel for the Market

If it's been years since you searched for work, you might not have a good grasp on the current market for the skills and experience that you bring. Since you began your last job, the country has gone through an explosion in the technology sector that drove compensation packages through the roof, and then a subsequent downturn that brought salaries back to reality. In the unsettled years since then, employers have modified wages and benefits to suit current conditions, creating a pretty broad range on both fronts.

Because you've been focused until now on advancing through the ranks of a single company, your compensation expectations could be unrealistic. The danger here is that the salary offers which you garner might fall seriously short of your expectations; that disappointment, in turn, could prevent you from recognizing a solid opportunity when it appears.

You can get a better feel for the market in several ways. First, scrutinize classified ads for positions in your field. You may not have particular interest in these positions, but where the jobs and employers are identified clearly, you'll gain some insight into the going rate for the type of role you're seeking.

Tap the knowledge of your friends and your network. It might be inappropriate to ask even a good friend, "How much do you make?" Instead, you might turn the question around so that it relates to you—something like: "I made $30,000 in my last job. What do you think I should look for now?" Almost invariably, your query will trigger a spirited discussion of salaries, as "who makes what" is a juicy topic that we all enjoy.

What you learn about current salaries won't be definitive—salary may be the most important element of any compensation package, but it's only one of many components that you'll weigh when considering offers. However, if you educate yourself about the current marketplace, you'll be well prepared to consider any offer that might emerge from an interview—and to plan a negotiating strategy if the climate is right.

46.

Going Backward?

For many, the sweetness of a job offer turns all too sour when they realize that the proposed salary is less than they earned in their previous positions. They think of this as "going backward," and in some cases conclude that their careers have peaked, since their wages are tumbling downhill. Now they're faced with a painful dilemma: to accept offers that they find offensive, or spurn them and submit to the uncertainties of a resumed job search.

This scenario can befall you if you regard your career as a financial progression with neat little steps up the compensation ladder, but this may be the wrong way to understand salary. Jobs should be evaluated on more criteria than wages alone. Benefits, opportunities for advancement, work environment, personal satisfaction—all are important characteristics of any position, and all can be as important as salary. What good are the big bucks if, for example, you find the work unfulfilling or you have to allocate your own funds to patch holes in the employer's health insurance? In

103

those cases, cashing that paycheck may leave you with a sense of irony rather than a glow of satisfaction.

The economy also plays a role in salaries. When a downturn displaces competent workers, a buyer's market is created for employers, who can lure talented people for less than they're used to paying for them. Your lowball offer may be no more than a reflection of a sagging economy rather than an indicator of your abilities. You're the same competent person that you always were, but the market may not be rewarding that competence very handsomely right now.

Get beyond the notion that you're a failure if your salary can't be plotted on an unbroken ascending line. If anything, you career should be a progression toward a broadening of your capabilities, an understanding of who you are and where you excel, and the fulfillment that comes with this self-actualization. A job that carries you along that path—no matter the salary—is a step forward.

47.

The Theory of Relativity, Job Style

As you pursue your new position, you may be dismayed initially if the salary that you're offered doesn't compare well with what you're accustomed to being paid. You're as skilled, as versatile, and as talented as you've ever been, so it seems logical that you should command a higher salary rather than accept a pay cut. You've run smack dab into the "theory of relativity, job style," where logic has little role.

The theory goes something like this: salary usually is relative to market conditions and needs and doesn't necessarily reflect employee capabilities. In a depressed market, salaries will decline because employers have diminished needs for high-priced staff and diminished willingness to pay for them.

You can view this latter-day theory of relativity in action all across our economy. Take the example of professional athletes in high-profile team sports—baseball, football, basketball, and hockey. Each of these sports witnessed dramatic market changes—specifically, the ability of players to move freely among teams within certain weak limitations. In a flash, athletes who once dreamed of $100,000 contracts were receiving millions, and it wasn't because they became overnight superstars, but rather that talent had become harder to retain.

The same effect, turned upside-down, is evident in the public safety field. We all regard the police officers who protect us as among our most vitally important professionals, yet you would never divine that information from police salaries, which don't compare well with those of athletes—or even the remuneration of many other professionals. The reason may be that in this era of bare-bones municipal budgets, the market has plenty of police—and candidates for those jobs. When the supply in a particular discipline is ample, it's difficult for the employees toiling in those vineyards to demand more.

If you appreciate relativity and its impact on your situation, you won't be offended by what you regard as inadequate salary offers. You can keep searching for better offers, or you can develop more realistic expectations consistent with the current market. In either case, low salary offers may result from changing market conditions, but they don't reflect your value as an employee and as a person. Those are absolute—never relative.

48.

Use All Available Resources

Companies forced to downsize by economic conditions often are aware of the hardships that separation may create for their former employees. Some even go so far as to offer services to help discharged staff in their search for new employment. This assistance can take a number of forms, including outplacement services, letters of recommendation, and use of company office space and support staff.

If you've been dismissed, your immediate response might be to spurn this offer of help. You're angry and hurt, and your pride is telling you that you don't need help from the firm that didn't appreciate you. While this is an understandable reaction to a traumatic event, it won't help your job search. When you managed a project for your former employer, you marshaled all of the resources that you could to accomplish the objective. You have an important new goal now—finding a position—and you'll need to gather and deploy every resource available.

Your downsizing likely was a rational, if painful, business decision. Now, you must be rational and businesslike in return. If outplacement services are offered, go to the initial meeting and evaluate the outplacement firm. If you determine that they can help you, go the next step with them. Your former employer is picking up the tab, so you have little to lose and something valuable to gain.

If your company offers a letter of recommendation, don't accept it passively. Work with them on the language. Make sure that the letter mentions your specific responsibilities, outstanding job performance, and promotions. You can develop a strong letter if you take a proactive position on its contents.

Don't hesitate to utilize the company's office space, if it's offered, as a temporary base for your search. Sure, it may be awkward to relate to people who only a few days ago were your colleagues, but most of them have been in your situation—or realize that they could be someday. Your relations with them will be as warm as ever, and they could become a valuable part of your job search network—yet another benefit of your former employer's resources.

49.

Understanding the Hiring Process

A t many companies, the hiring process can be elaborate, if not downright Byzantine. You may think that meeting with the hiring manager will be your only audition, or that, at most, you'll have one more meeting with a department head if you survive the first cut. Often, though, this is far from the case.

The sluggish economy that we endured early in this century brought a wave of downsizings that inspired employers to identify and recruit *exactly* the right people for their needs. No longer can they afford long learning curves; no longer can they afford personnel mistakes. This emphasis on effective hiring is reflected in processes that involve more time, more people, and more meetings.

In the technology sector, for example, it's not unusual for young companies to invite candidates in for an entire day of meetings with prospective colleagues. Since hours are demanding and the work environment is intense at growing tech firms, they want to determine as best they can if applicants will develop the appropriate "chemistry" with current employees.

For you, these developments mean that the hiring process may be lengthier and more involved than you imagined. You certainly won't get any glimpse into the process from classified ads, nor will hiring managers always be up front with you about the number of interviews that you may face or the executives that you must meet.

During your interview, it's reasonable for you to inquire about the process. You have a schedule to map out, and it's only fair for you to know how many rounds of callbacks they may be planning and, if there's travel involved, how long you might be expected to be away from home. Travel, by the way, is more likely if you're interviewing with the local office of a company that's headquartered elsewhere. They may well want you to meet with appropriate executives in the home office, and it's nearly certain that those chieftains won't be flying in to see you.

Try asking about the hiring process this way: "I wonder if you could share the entire hiring process with me. I want to make sure that I'm available when you need me." If you structure your inquiry this way, you may get the information you want, while earning points for being considerate.

50.

Integrity Is the Thing

I t's hard to turn on the news these days without hearing of another high-profile CEO forced to acknowledge financial improprieties. You may feel mild dismay about the decline of ethics but shrug off the news otherwise; it seems light-years removed from your daily concerns. It isn't, though. We all face moral dilemmas, no matter the size of our paychecks or our roles in society. You're a CEO now—the chief executive officer of your own job search—so you're likely to encounter some challenging ethical questions along the way.

The first set of tough calls may involve your resume preparation. As you review your accomplishments, you may not consider them strong enough and so may be tempted to embellish them. You also may get into a moral bind at the unemployment benefits office, particularly if you're earning part-time income as you search for full-time work. You know that the right thing is to report all income, but that could result in a commensurate reduction in your unemployment compensation at a time when you really need it.

Then there are job interviews, where each question can be a stern test of your moral probity. Answer the questions honestly, and you may fear that you won't make a lasting impression. Stretch your achievements a little, and you could be crossing that moral divide.

Under ordinary circumstances, you wouldn't have any trouble selecting the ethical course of action in all these cases, but the pressures of a job search can be anything but ordinary. They can turn black-and-white issues a murky shade of gray.

How can you always be sure that you will choose wisely? Simply by remembering that maintaining your integrity is as important as landing the right position. Jobs come and go with the economy; integrity is for a lifetime. Make the right choices throughout your search, and everyone you encounter will know that you're a CEO—a completely ethical operator.

51.

About Those Gaps in Your Resume

Your resume looks great, showing all the responsible positions that you've held and how responsibly you executed them. It looks great, that is, until you get to those gaps, those periods of months or years when you were without work. As you deal with the uncertainties and frustrations of your job search, you magnify those gaps in your own mind until they become chasms, unbridgeable by even the most sympathetic hiring manager.

If your resume illustrates interrupted work cycles, the first thing that you should do about it is relax. Keep resume gaps in the proper perspective. Almost everyone realizes that the jittery economy of recent years has brought dislocations for workers with otherwise solid records of accomplishment. Rare is the person who hasn't faced downsizing or suffered through it with a friend or loved one.

Hiring managers and department heads are no exceptions. In fact, HR professionals appreciate better than most that cutbacks can catch even the most capable of workers. They know the numbers game pretty well, and they're unlikely to assign too much weight to brief periods of unemployment—provided that the resume otherwise indicates competence and reliability. You're quite likely to find understanding in this group.

Also, it's probably wise to resist the temptation to invent activities that would appear to cover your employment gaps. If you were self-employed during those periods, it's appropriate to say so. If you were freelancing, it's okay to mention that, too. However, if you weren't legitimately involved in these pursuits, don't stretch reality, or you may face some embarrassing questions about these periods. The whole web could unravel in a moment, leaving you substantially worse off than you were before.

Treat gaps in your resume with straightforward answers and integrity, as you do all other aspects of your employment and personal history. You're a strong candidate with much to offer. When you confront resume gaps honestly, prospective employers will realize that they have the opportunity to hire a person who's long on candor. When that happens, you'll have transformed a seeming liability into a valuable asset.

52.

Some Tips on Resumes

What an amazing adventure resume preparation is! Your resume may not be the most important document that you prepare during your life, but it probably is the most significant artifact of your job search. If a stranger asked you to encapsulate your career and personal life in a few paragraphs, you wouldn't know where to begin—or where to end. Yet that's just what we're asked to do on our resumes: summarize our professional and personal history, and—oh, yes—keep it to one page, please.

Because resumes are so vital and so challenging, HR experts have written a great deal about successful preparation. In some cases, though, even the experts don't agree. If you find yourself frustrated by conflicting advice, it may be best to adopt a common-sense approach and apply it to these "truisms" about resumes.

Resumes should be no longer than one page. The thinking here is that busy hiring managers don't have the time to read more than a single page and might even toss anything longer than that in the round file. Yes, resumes should be compact, but not at the expense of content. If you've enjoyed a lengthy career, rich with accomplishment, you won't be able to squeeze all of that onto a single page—and you might omit achievements that readers would consider impressive.

Resumes should be printed on eye-catching paper. Bold colors will grab the hiring manager's attention, this theory goes, and it may have some validity. However, vividness also may raise the reader's expectations. If the content isn't as bright as the color, this ploy will do you little good.

Highlights of your resume should be emphasized. This is solid common sense. If hiring managers are skimming your resume, they'll be drawn to any material that's physically emphasized, so use a bigger font and boldface for your career and personal peaks. That may propel readers to a more thorough examination of your paperwork.

We often think of hiring managers as an undifferentiated type; they're far from that, and they respond to resumes as individuals. What some regard as attractive will be dismissed by others as a cheap trick, so think less about the audience and more about what you want to convey. Then your compelling resume will speak for itself.

53.

Hire a Pro or Do It Yourself?

If you've assembled and produced your resume yourself, chances are that you've created an outstanding document. When friends in your job network mention that they've hired professionals to prepare their resumes, however, you may feel anxious and wonder if the do-it-yourself approach will be a strike against you.

While the pressures of your job search may magnify the importance of this issue, there are factors to consider in resume development. Graphic design professionals may help you shape a distinctive resume. A commercial print shop can give your resume a polished look that you might not be able to achieve at your desktop. These are the advantages of engaging outside help, but there are drawbacks, as well.

For one, a designer may be able to provide an attractive and appropriate format for your resume, but your consultant won't know what career information to include—or which jobs and achievements to emphasize—without significant input from you. When

117

you outsource your resume, you also become dependent, to a greater or lesser degree, on the schedules of your consultants. If they prioritize assignments from larger clients and relegate you to the back burner, you may not have your resumes when you need them. At that point, it won't matter how sharp they look—or would have looked, had you been able to coax them from your printer.

There's also the matter of cost, a not-insignificant item when financial resources are tight. When you were employed, you might have thought nothing about an expenditure of two hundred dollars—a typical cost for resume development and printing. Now, you and your family could find two hundred useful ways to spend that two hundred dollars.

The bottom line in this area of your job search is that you need to do whatever it takes to produce a resume that reads well and looks credible. If you can accomplish this task yourself, do it, and don't worry about what others may be doing. If you need some outside help, bring it on board, and consider the money well-spent. You'll be repaid many times over when that resume helps you land a terrific job.

54.

Refer to Your References

Imagine that you're a hiring manager. You're reviewing the resume of a candidate who appears to have the right competencies and experience when you come upon the heading "References." Here, the candidate has written: "Available upon request." Your response to this bit of deliberate mystery is not likely to be favorable. After all, if the references were strong, wouldn't the applicant have included them?

While the practice of shielding references seems to have dubious merit, many applicants practice it routinely. Perhaps it's because they haven't taken the trouble to solicit appropriate referrals, or they think that this will tempt hiring managers to pursue their references and give their resumes additional consideration. It could also be that they have not yet alerted those people that they would like to list as references. Maybe the real motivation, after all, is the most obvious one—applicants are vague about their references because they don't consider them strong or persuasive enough.

Given the popularity of this practice, you may gain a considerable edge by specifying your references. List their names, titles, employers, business addresses, and phone numbers so that hiring managers can follow up if they choose. Of course, you'll want to gain authorization from your references before providing any of this information. You don't want someone you cite as a reference to be surprised by a phone call from a hiring manager; in that unrehearsed situation, you never know what a colleague or former supervisor might say. Get specific approval from your references, and let them know that they might be receiving phone calls about you.

You also can enhance your resume package with letters of referral. If colleagues or former employers are willing to write brief letters on your behalf, encourage them to be as detailed as possible, and to include the specific areas of your career—including responsibilities and performance—with which they're familiar. Testimony about specific accomplishments is much more helpful than general endorsements of your character.

A great thing about creating a strong references section of your resume is that you're saving hiring managers time and effort. They don't have to track down referrals for you—you've provided them in an attractive, accessible format. That's bound to be a strong point in your favor.

55.

Appearance Is Not a Dealbreaker

When we make the rounds of interviews, we worry more than ever about the way we look. Our thinking is that hiring managers are searching for anything that will help them remember applicants positively—or disqualify them from further consideration—so the first impression that we make on interviewers is critically important. This thinking is not entirely illogical. Hiring managers often are hard-pressed to distinguish among all of the worthy candidates they're interviewing, so they may fall back on appearance to help get them to the next round.

However, even the most superficial interviewer quickly gets beyond appearances to more substantive matters, such as how you're likely to perform on the job. Given this, you may not want to worry unduly about your appearance. Of course, you want to look presentable, but that's hardly a challenge for you. You're used to operating in the business world, and looking your best is second nature to you—but you still may worry about those style points that help you express your personality.

If you have a beard, for example, will an interviewer regard you as an extreme individualist rather than a team player? Will an ear stud make you appear over-the-top to an old-line, conservative company? Will a distinctive coiffure stamp you as a potential troublemaker in the eyes of an older generation?

While there's a remote chance that the answer to any of these questions will be "yes," it's far more likely that interviewers will be interested in the real you. That's what you want to showcase in every interview—your skills, experience, and personality strengths. Your appearance isn't necessarily a clue to any of those elements, so interviewers won't dwell on how you look. Once you're sure you cut an appropriately professional figure, don't fret about your appearance beyond that. When you feel good about how you look, your personality will flash brightly. That, more than your appearance, is what interviewers will remember.

56.

Your "Hire Attire"

We all like to look our best for job interviews. Even in this more relaxed era, when the stuffiest blue-chip companies have stripped away their strict dress codes and gone casual, we know that hiring managers may be giving our attire the once-over. It makes more than a little sense to dress for success—but you can overdo your attention to this one small facet of your job search. What we wear is nothing more than packaging; what companies are looking for most keenly is product—that is to say, the real you.

The impact of packaging usually is limited. At the supermarket, you may be attracted to items with colorful wrappers. You may be moved to pick up these items and read their ingredient labels. Ultimately, though, what you purchase are the products that most please you, despite what the containers look like. In the same way, your clothing may briefly pique the interest of hiring managers, but what seals the deal are your talents, your experience, and your personality.

There's also the matter of expense. It's reasonable to enhance your wardrobe a bit as an aid to your search. It's unreasonable to spring for a new suit or outfit for each interview, particularly if you purchase your new threads with plastic. That's debt that you don't need, and it's probably quite unnecessary. Chances are that you'll look just fine in clothes that are already hanging in your closet.

Still another drawback of wearing your best clothes to every interview is that you may look sharp but feel flat. Think about those dressy shoes that you haul out of the closet and polish to a shine for parties. Remember how badly they pinch your feet, how you sometimes escape to the restroom to slip them off for a few moments' relief? In an interview, how alert will your responses be when you're distracted by a pair of aching feet?

A useful practice here may be to look good—and you always do—but not at the expense of comfort. When you feel strong and confident, the real you will emerge every time.

57.

The Interview—Play It Straight

The best thing to be in an interview is you. When you're confident and forthcoming, all of your strengths will be apparent to the interviewer, and you'll be well on your way to establishing the rapport that many hiring managers regard as crucial for further consideration.

In the heat of the moment, though, you may forget the relaxed, natural approach and attempt to verbally embellish your job record or reach for accomplishments that aren't really there. This can be an especially seductive temptation if you sense that the session isn't going well. Perhaps you notice a suggestive frown, a scratch of the head—or the interviewer leafs through your resume with a puzzled or dubious expression. Does this mean that you're on the verge of rejection? You'll do anything to prevent that, even blurt out an exaggerated claim to keep the interview alive.

This is a dangerous overreaction. Many interviewers adopt a professional mien, a "game face," if you will, that they've developed just to prevent you from reading them. They may want to control the interview, keep you at a distance, and see how you react to this pressure. Trying to read their body language is tricky at best, and it may lead you down the path to exaggeration.

Remember that a sharp hiring manager has the tools to verify most claims. Your resume is one resource that's readily available—you've already provided it if you get to the interview stage. If, in the heat of moment, you allow that you ran a twenty-million-dollar department, your chances for this job may be seriously compromised if your resume doesn't support your assertion.

Checking with your references is yet another way for interviewers to verify contentions that don't ring true. This is the worst of all possible worlds; your claim can't be substantiated, and you've placed a trusted friend in an embarrassing position.

All of this suggests that you must resist any pressure to put a better face on your career accomplishments. That doesn't mean that you must remain passive or matter-of-fact in interviews. When you want to go beyond an interviewer's question, when you feel genuine enthusiasm for the topic, let it show. That's more likely to create a favorable impression than dubious claims, and you'll retain your all-important credibility.

58.

Overcoming Intimidation

Interviews are unsettling. The very notion that you're auditioning for a job is scary enough, but just about everything that happens that day can contribute to your queasiness. You drive to a building which you've never entered before and you aren't sure where to park. As you sit in the lobby waiting for your appointment, you see dozens of happy, confident people walking the halls, casting your misery in an even harsher light.

You're asked whether you want something to drink; even this simple question sends you into a tizzy. Is it more appropriate to accept or decline? Then when it's finally time for your interview, you sit at the petitioner's end of a big desk, knowing that you'll be grilled by a veteran with all the answers, while you have none.

If this is the way that you've begun to perceive interviews, you've let the intimidation factor get to you. This is not to minimize the stress that job interviews may produce, but if you remember just how talented and experienced you are, you'll keep that pressure at a manageable level. You're a strong candidate for this job, and you bring a lot to the table. If that weren't the case, why would they have agreed to see you?

When summoned by the King of Siam, Anna whistled a happy tune to keep from being overwhelmed by the situation. Whistling through the halls of a corporation might not be the ideal stress reliever these days, but how about going online prior to your interview to learn something about the company? Review their web site. Take a look at what they say about their products, personnel, and customer service operations. Not only will that familiarity provide a comfort level for your interview, but your new understanding of the company might help you formulate key questions.

If your preparedness makes you feel like puckering up, go ahead, give in to the urge—for a few bars, anyway. You've overcome the intimidation factor, and that's worth whistling about.

59.

Off-the-Wall Interview Questions

B eing interviewed for jobs can be a stressful grind. You're certain that every word, every gesture will be intensely scrutinized, and that one slip will be enough to disqualify you. Of course, you've exaggerated the scenario in your own mind, but that's what the pressures of interviewing can do.

You may be comforted by the realization that on the other side of the table, it's not always peaches and cream. Interviewers, too, have their work cut out for them. They must identify that one great candidate from so many who look promising, but when they review the notes from all of their interviews, they may find little to distinguish the applicants. In these challenging situations, they may turn to off-the-wall—or even bizarre—questions to elicit responses that will help them differentiate among candidates.

So there you are, rolling along smoothly, knocking all the softballs out of the park, when the hiring manager looks you in the eye and asks, "If you were a tree, what type of tree would you be?"

Perhaps the question deals with professional matters but is no less surprising for that, something like: "If two people in your department began dating, what would your response be?"

Perhaps the most unfair aspect of such oddball questions is that they don't appear to measure your capabilities in any useful way. Certainly, unusual situations can arise on the job, but rare is the incident that requires a split-second, seat-of-the-pants reaction—as you are now being asked to provide.

So if you're confronted by strange questions, the wisest course of action may be to request a little time to mull over the possibilities before responding. On the job, you would do much the same thing—gather information, confer with colleagues—before taking any action. Your conduct would be thorough and measured. Take the same tack here. Your interviewer should be impressed with your thoughtful approach.

60.

Should You Interview Them?

Job interviews should be easy. At their most basic level, they're no more than two people conversing—something that we do every day of our lives. Of course, when these pleasant little chats are transformed into formal job interviews, we feel that familiar queasiness in our stomachs and search desperately for the right style to adopt.

Because interviews are both important and stressful, placement services offer considerable advice on the most persuasive interview behavior. Surprisingly, their counsel is far from consistent. Some experts suggest a nearly passive approach, providing name-rank-serial-number-type answers without straying too far afield. Don't ask too many questions, they recommend, lest the hiring manager judge you to be too interested in yourself and not a reliable team player.

Others advise a more assertive style: volunteer answers that are well beyond the scope of the questions, and ask a slew of questions yourself. The thinking here is that interviewers will mark you highly for your energy and independence, and that will put you a cut above your more quiescent rivals.

The common denominator in this confusing clutter is perception; in each case, you're advised to be concerned about how an inquisitive posture might appear to hiring managers. No doubt, this is relevant—yet a more important outcome for you is getting all of the information that you need. Hiring managers want to evaluate you, but you also have an evaluation to make of each prospective employer. For that, you must have your key questions answered.

Don't hesitate to ask those questions. Ask about the benefits package and any particular features that may apply to you and your family. Find out about probation periods. Explore career paths that may be open to you. If you can, determine all of the steps in the hiring process so that you can schedule them appropriately.

Weave your questions throughout the interview as deftly as you can, but if you find that you must cluster them at the very end of the session, fire away. When you get the information that you need, you'll be well-positioned to make an effective decision.

61.

This Has Been a Test

As you interview for jobs, you may find that hiring managers require you to submit to tests—not drug tests, which happen more or less routinely these days before hiring can commence, but aptitude or skills tests. The theory is that these drills will provide hiring managers with a concrete way of measuring your abilities and help them distinguish among all applicants. In practice, however, job testing leaves a lot to be desired.

For years, one of the most widely used job exams was the in-box test. Applicants would be seated at a desk. There, they would find an in-box cluttered with memos, directives, and assorted other communications. Their assignment—accomplish as much as they could within a set time period. Typically, hiring managers would bury a critical task beneath a pile of extraneous stuff, wanting to see if applicants would take the time to sort through all of the material and prioritize the chores. Those who did received high marks; those who didn't were shown the out-box.

In-box tests are devilishly clever, but do they effectively measure your abilities? In a real-life situation, you would have plenty of other cues regarding the importance and time-sensitivity of your assignments, and you would have plenty of additional resources to tap—such as your colleagues. None of your consensus-building skills would be useful or visible in the test.

Tests also are popular with news organizations. Applicants may be given copy that's chock full of errors and asked to correct the text. That's fine, as far as it goes, but at a real news desk, you wouldn't need to know everything off the top of your head. You would have resources—dictionaries, style books, old clippings—that you could consult. Knowing things is important; knowing how and where to find things may be even more vital, and tests of this sort won't measure that.

Job tests, in short, may not measure what they're supposed to measure, and what they do measure may not be relevant to performance. Nevertheless, tests are a fact of life, so you must build the expectation of job tests into your search. You can't prepare or study for them, so don't stress about them. Accept these challenges eagerly. Bring your customary talent and creativity to job tests, and you'll ace them every time.

62.

Following Up Without Overdoing It

As you fill out applications, submit resumes, and interview for jobs, it's hard not to feel antsy. Your career is on hold while prospective new employers consider you, and you'd like to get their answer yesterday. Of course, employers may not feel quite the same urgency, so their responses may be slower in coming. In these circumstances, a delay of only a day or two may seem interminable.

When this happens—when the gap between your resume submission or interview and the decision appears unreasonably long—you may want to follow up with a phone call to the hiring manager. This is quite a reasonable thing for you to do, given everything that's riding on the outcome. Most hiring managers understand your anxiety, and they'll take a minute to update you on the process.

A danger in following up, though, is overdoing it. If hiring managers don't respond immediately to your first phone call, you may feel compelled to pepper their offices with voicemail until they do get back to you. Ordinarily, this overeagerness—natural as it may seem to you—won't work in your favor.

135

Put yourself in the position of hiring managers. These harried, overworked executives have endured a grueling day putting out fires and battling corporate dragons, only to return to the office and find five messages from you. It's not hard to imagine their customary congeniality turning to mild annoyance—or worse.

A better approach is to familiarize yourself with the hiring process at its outset. Get an understanding of when the decision will be made. If you're advised that the selection is a week to ten days away, you'll be less anxious during that period when you're in limbo.

This doesn't mean that you can't stay in touch. Pick out a nice greeting card for the hiring manager. Append a handwritten note indicating your appreciation at being considered. It's a nice, low-key way of demonstrating your thoughtfulness and your continuing interest in the position—without overdoing it.

63.

Don't Take It Personally

If you're one of the lucky few who finds success with that first application or interview, you won't have to endure the pain of rejection. For most of us, though, the quest will last longer than one application, which means we will be rejected.

No matter what form rejection takes, it's a blow to your pride and self-esteem. If an employer fails to respond to your application or resume, that's an impersonal brush-off that's as frustrating as it is painful; you're not even sure where to direct your anger, since you may have corresponded only with a post office box.

Remember that in most cases, the prospective employer's action had little to do with you personally. In the early phases of recruitment and hiring, most managers are able to pay only cursory attention to the hundreds of applications they receive. They couldn't possibly come to know you personally, so there's nothing personal in their rejection of you.

On other occasions, jobs will have been filled by the time your resume hits the hiring manager's desk. In these cases, you really haven't been rejected at all, since no opportunity was available by the time you were up for consideration.

Worse still are situations where you make it through the first few phases, only to fail when that offer seems tantalizingly close. Now, rejection threatens to become very personal. You know that the employer became familiar with your credentials—and rejected you anyway.

Even when you reach a second or third round of interviews before falling, the news here is more positive than negative. The company thought so much of you that it kept calling you back for further evaluation. True, they didn't tender an offer to you, but from an entire universe of possible employees, you were among a tiny handful that passed muster for final consideration. That should reinforce your confidence and optimism about your search.

It's important to keep rejection from becoming dejection, which could be a bigger blow to your job search than anything. Perhaps that can serve as a job search mantra—"Rejected, not dejected."

64.

If You Come Up Short, Ask Why

O ne of the most bewildering aspects of any job search is what might be thought of as the unspecified rejection—you're not called back for an interview or second session, you don't get the offer, and no one will tell you why.

As cold as this may seem, it's understandable in some situations— particularly those that involve hundreds of applications or interviews. Providing detailed explanations along with rejections would be beyond the capabilities of most hiring managers and companies, so there's little point in getting worked up about such rejections.

However, when you've had an interview or two, you've met with senior management and prospective colleagues, and you still get only a form rejection, that really hurts. What's more, the rejection is of little value to you—you learn nothing from it— because you haven't been advised where you came up short.

When this happens, it's worth your time and energy to pursue the details. If you can, get in touch with the hiring manager or department head involved. This won't always be easy, as few executives are particularly eager to chat with rejected applicants. Some will take your call, though, and some will explain their hiring decisions, if you ask politely enough.

You have valuable information now, but don't overreact. Review it, save it, and compare it to other evaluations that you receive along the way. You're in a great position to determine how others perceive your personality, skills, and work record, and whether there's any difference between that perception and your image of yourself.

It's possible that none of this data will lead you to any insights about yourself. Then again, if three prospective employers cite inadequate skills in a key area, those who rejected you may be giving you a road map to a training program—and future success in your job search.

65.

Stay in Control

Your job search will begin as a clean, uncomplicated journey. You know what you want, and you know how to get it—what could be simpler than that? As you get deeper into your search, however, you may find that mounting tasks and pressures, coupled with family responsibilities and financial worries, transform your straight-line search into a hydra-headed monster.

So many tasks demand your attention that it's hard to know which to perform first. If you're like most of us, you'll gravitate to the easiest tasks and save the more demanding chores for "later"—some unspecified time in the future when the pace slows. You may, for example, opt to review online job sources as your first task of the day because it's a relatively painless duty. You don't have to fight your way through the thicket of some company's tangled phone menu—and no web site will burst your bubble with words of rejection. This aspect of your quest may not be as critical as following up job interviews, but you know that rejection may be lurking there, so you postpone those phone calls until "later." Of course, "later" may never actually arrive, leaving certain tasks dangling. If there's timely business in that list of tasks that you've been putting off, key opportunities may be lost.

To avoid this, work hard to stay in control when the pace turns a little frantic. Here's where a firm understanding of your goals will help you retain a sense of normalcy and progress. When you know what you want to achieve, you'll be better able to prioritize the possible courses of action before you.

Perform the most important tasks first, even if they leave you feeling a little queasy. As time permits, you'll get to the less significant items on your list—but if time doesn't permit, chances are that you won't be ignoring tasks that could have a major impact on your search. When you're confident that you've ordered your tasks properly, you'll regain that feeling of being in control.

66.

Review Hiring Documents Carefully

When you secure that great new position, you have an important task before you—careful review of the new-hire package. This may not be high on your list, as you'll be particularly eager to learn your new job responsibilities and get acquainted with your colleagues, but a careful read of hiring documents should be a priority. Tucked away in these often-numbing documents are the policies and practices that could set the tone for your tenure with your new employer.

Dig into the benefits package right away. When you were interviewing for the position, you likely touched on the highlights with the hiring manager. Now that you have enrollment decisions to make, understanding the details is most important.

Go through the health plan options to determine rates and scope of coverage. If your spouse is enrolled in a plan, compare costs and features, and see which plan makes more sense for your family. Look also at other types of insurance. Are life insurance and disability insurance offered? If so, do they provide adequate levels of coverage, or will you need to supplement them with private policies? These are issues to be resolved sooner rather than later.

Your package may include an employee manual and a company code of conduct. In light of recent accounting scandals, many companies have developed these documents to articulate what they consider acceptable behavior—and what they demand of employees in matters of ethics. Their expectations cover new hires and probationary employees, so familiarizing yourself with company culture is a must.

If you use a computer at the office, you'll need to understand the company's policy on computer and e-mail use. This is a relatively new wrinkle—a product of the information age that may not have surfaced the last time that you were hired. For example, you may want to fire off an e-mail to your family right away to let them know how things are going, but does your employer permit personal e-mail? Are you free to erase e-mail, or must you preserve all electronic communications? You won't know if you don't study the policy.

None of this should diminish your enthusiasm for your new job. Chances are excellent that it will work out just as you envisioned. However, you'll improve those chances even more by treating your new-hire package in a timely fashion rather than relegating it to the back burner.

67.

On Probationary Periods

An offer for the perfect job is definitely cause for celebration, yet you still have that final mile to go before you're home free—the probationary period. Most employers of any size impose probationary periods on new hires. The length of probation may vary—three months to six months is typical—and other terms, as well, may be company-specific. What makes these trials somewhat worrisome is that evaluation of probationary employees generally is at the complete discretion of employers. If they don't carry you past your probation, they're not required to explain why. Probationary employees have the full responsibilities of other staff, but not necessarily the full rights package.

Probation is a product of the uncertainties of the recruitment and hiring process. Although employers take elaborate measures to select exactly the right employees, they're still not sure if they've made good hires. Probation is their backstop. It's not directed against you personally, of course, yet there's very little that you can do to avoid this trial. Even if your credentials are stellar, most employers won't waive or shorten probation, lest they be required to do so for other staff.

One thing that you *can* do is become fully conversant with the terms of your probation. Will you be paid your full salary and have access to vacation days, sick days, and personal days during your probation? Will you receive periodic evaluations, and by whom? Does the company provide coaching if you encounter problems? You need answers to these questions before you can fully assess your job offer.

When you're comfortable with the details, you're ready to turn this lemon into lemonade. Take your probationary period and transform it into a showcase for your skills, energy, and team play. Go beyond what's expected of new hires. You'll pass your probation with flying colors, and make an indelible first impression on your new employer and colleagues.

68.

The Chemistry Thing

When they recruit, hiring managers and department heads often find little to distinguish the applicants before them. All of the candidates seem to bring the requisite skills. All have excellent resumes and credible references, and all were sharp enough during their interviews. Rather than toss a coin—a practice that likely would be frowned on by their professional peers—hiring managers often turn to that mysterious dynamic known as "chemistry."

"We like your credentials," they might tell you by way of rejection, "but the chemistry just wasn't there." What they seem to mean here is that they didn't perceive the development of an instant rapport between you and them, and that when they project this to the job site, you might not have the right chemistry with the staff, either. The smaller the company, the more likely it is to cite bad chemistry as a disqualifying factor; relationships in these firms often are more intense, so chemistry is regarded even more highly.

Sympathetic as we all should be to hiring managers, some may seem to rely too much on chemistry. Job interviews are inherently stressful. As such, they can be unreliable indicators of overall amiability and compatibility. Moreover, if interviewers don't feel that warm surge of chemistry with you, maybe the fault lies on their end of the table, and not yours.

The chemistry thing is exasperating; the first time you hear it, you know that you never want to hear it again. It's not something for which you can prepare, not a behavior that you can practice or modify, not even a factor that hiring managers could define if pressed—but there it is, costing you a chance.

Perhaps the best approach to chemistry is to forget it. Be your usual genial self in job interviews, and whatever chemistry is, it will develop more often than not. Remember that some of the most successful people in the world flunked chemistry.

69.

Keeping the Pressure Off

If you awaken with a sense of dread because you know that the day will bring another round of fruitless applications, superficial interviews, and impersonal rejections; if you can't bear explaining your circumstances to even one more well-wisher; if the prospect of laboring through the unemployment benefits phone menu fills with you anxiety—you know it's time for a break. It's perfectly normal to experience this sort of midseason slump. Job searches are packed with unavoidable pressures that affect even those with the most upbeat outlook. Pressure becomes perilous if unrelieved, so it's important for you to get that relief.

The ideal break would be a nice weekend away. Your destination needn't be anyplace too distant—just far enough away that you're focusing on pleasurable pastimes rather than your bulging job search folder. Include your family if you can. Remember, they feel every bump and bruise of your search as deeply as you do, so they may need a vacation from the tension as well.

Perhaps your financial situation won't allow a full-fledged getaway. If that's the case, bring some creativity to the task. Put together a few back-to-back day trips. You might visit a local landmark that somehow you've missed in your travels, or a rustic inn that your family will enjoy. The zoo, museums, sporting events, a drive through the countryside—all can transport you and your loved ones away from your job search for a little while.

When you resume your quest, you'll find that several wonderful things have happened. You'll be infinitely more relaxed and ready to slay the job search monsters once more. You may also find yourself positively bursting with new strategies to implement, and new ideas to run by friends and advisors. One of the oddities of human nature is that the closer we get to a problem, the less likely we are to perceive the solution. With your freshened perspective, you'll get a clear view of the forest—and the trees.

70.

Straight Talk for Your Kids

Telling your kids that you've lost your job is never easy. It's a setback for all of the members of your family, of course, but it can be especially tough on the little ones, as children tend to identify closely with their parents' occupations.

Kids are fond of boasting about you to their playmates. With pride they say, "My mom is a doctor" or "My dad is an engineer." If Mom or Dad is no longer working as a doctor or engineer—no longer has any job, in fact—how will your kids participate in this youthful one-upmanship? The situation can be especially confusing for them if you've taken your child to work as part of that national movement. You're no longer part of that professional environment now, and your kids may have a hard time understanding why.

Most children have yet to appreciate that our occupations, however important they may be, don't define us. We're the complex products of our actions, our words, our personalities, our experiences, and all of the influences that have helped to shape us. Your kids might

151

not be ready to grasp that yet, but now is a good time to help them on the way to this very adult insight.

Explain to your kids what has happened in your career. Let them know that all of their basic needs will be provided for. Help them remain upbeat by sharing with them your plans for your job search. Answer their questions in a straightforward way. Above all, remind them that nothing has altered your relationship with them—that will always be a source of fulfillment for all of you.

If your children don't get it all at once, don't be alarmed. They may need some time to absorb this unprecedented development, but they'll come around. You can speed this process by involving them in your job search. For example, your search may have a substantial online component that includes compiling research on target companies, visiting employment web sites, and downloading materials. Assign your kids some of these tasks. Given their nascent computer skills, they may do even more than you requested. Not only will they become more comfortable with the family's new situation, but they'll become valuable assets in your search.

71.

Easing Your Parents' Worries

One of your most important goals as you conduct your search will be maintaining and supporting the optimism of those closest to you. When they're confident about your prospects, you'll draw positive energy from them. Your spouse will be a natural source of encouragement, and your children, with their resilience and buoyancy, will be contributing members of the team in no time flat.

A bigger challenge may be easing the fears of your parents. No one worries more about you than they do; they'll worry about your financial situation, your state of mind, and when and where you'll ultimately find work. Their moods can rise and fall alarmingly with each application and interview. Their concern may be aggravated if your job loss took them by surprise.

One way to keep them from worrying unduly is to bring them into the information loop as soon as possible. For instance, if you know that you work in a turbulent industry where mergers, acquisitions, or failures could cost you your job, make them aware of the possibility.

At the same time, it's important to let them know that you're financially secure enough to ride out the storm, and that your chances for a new job are excellent. Should the worst come to pass, they'll be buffered by your timely explanation.

Advise them also that you may be seeking unemployment compensation—if you're eligible. They may be part of a generation that tends to view such compensation as degrading—something for other people, perhaps, but not for their own children. With some gentle coaching, you can help them update their outmoded view.

When parents offer to help, accept their generosity. If you don't need their financial assistance, let them know that, but make sure they're aware that you're counting on them if the need arises. Keep them posted on the broad sweep of your search—not every detail, but the highlights. They'll be gratified and reassured when they know that good things are happening.

Then when your parents clip want ads from the newspaper and send them to you, as loving parents will do, don't dismiss these leads out of hand. Follow up those that are appropriate, and let your folks know that you've done so. They'll be thrilled to be part of your search.

72.

Unemployment Is Not Contagious

It was only a few generations ago that unemployment seemed as embarrassing as a social disease. We didn't want to catch it, we didn't want to discuss it, and we certainly didn't want to be seen mingling with the victims of this professional malady. There was widespread belief that if you lost your job, you must have deserved it. Companies didn't dismiss competent employees, did they? If they fired you, you must be a loser.

Over the past several decades, we've learned that this stereotype is outdated. Employers lay off their employees for all sorts of reasons, with poor company performance perhaps the leading cause. Realizing this at last, we've all developed greater empathy for those temporarily out of work.

Perhaps the last barrier to the elimination of this stereotype forever is the lingering uncertainty that unemployment has raised in your own mind. At one level, you realize that you're a valuable, dignified member of society. At a deeper level, you may harbor doubts

155

about yourself. If you catch yourself hanging back at parties and other social events, afraid to mix and mingle lest the conversation turn to your job search, you know that you're still clinging to vestiges of the old stereotype.

Step up to the conversational plate. Talk about your situation comfortably. The more you do so, the more matter-of-fact you'll become about discussing your job search. You'll be amazed at how understanding and helpful people will be. However, don't let your job search dominate the conversation. You're a multifaceted person with wide-ranging interests that are more entertaining than status reports on applications and interviews. Introduce some of these other topics to balance out the interaction.

You can apply these same lessons when you encounter someone else on a job search. You know that your new friend will value any leads and concrete advice you can offer but isn't looking for pity. Discuss the employment situation, and then ease into other topics of mutual interest. Agreeable conversation can be full of fascinating surprises; neither your job search nor anyone else's should keep you from discovering them.

73.

Get Out There and—Party!

You've brought an admirable single-mindedness to your job search, devoting just about every waking minute to identifying and pursuing the right opportunities. There comes a time, however, when this doggedness can have diminishing returns. If your relentlessness threatens to wear you out—physically and psychologically—it may be time to step away from it for awhile and socialize.

Socializing can take many forms. You can have lunch with your spouse. You can activate your job network for an evening of comparing notes. You might even drop in on a couple of parties. In moderation, socializing will help you relax. When you continue your job search, you'll do so with renewed vigor and optimism.

Socializing also can aid your job prospects. You may encounter people who have job leads or professional contacts for you. When you exchange business cards with them, you'll actually be working on your search and relaxing at the same time. So go ahead and let loose for an evening—and keep a few resumes in the car, just in case.

74.

Part-Time Gigs

While focusing on their quest for full-time jobs, some folks shun part-time work for fear that it will distract them or otherwise impede their searches. This is a legitimate concern. However, if you can land part-time jobs or projects that don't interfere with your search, they can be a valuable source of income and self-affirmation.

A fruitful source for part-time work may be your former employer—assuming that the lines of communication are open there. Check out the possibility of consulting or project assignments for your old company. Also, go through your business cards and address book to see which of your old professional contacts might have part-time work available. After so many waves of downsizing, many businesses don't have enough employees remaining to handle all of the tasks that must be done. They might welcome the opportunity to tap your expertise on a part-time basis.

The great thing about part-time work within your field is that you're expanding your contacts in your discipline—and you'll come away with a great credit for your resume. Who knows? When you bring your characteristic drive and creativity to a part-time gig, it could yield an offer of a permanent position. What a happy ending to your search that would be!

If no part-time gigs are available in your discipline, accept any work that you can handle, as long as it is work that brings you some satisfaction and productive interaction with others. Certainly, establishing an income stream is a primary goal of part-time work, but an equally important objective is helping you retain your sense of purpose and worth as you contribute to a team effort. You won't get that from a job that's pure drudgery.

Remember, too, that at tax time, you must report your wages from part-time jobs, just as you do all other income. Since they're enduring tough times, some part-time workers try to skirt this requirement, figuring that they need every dollar they can muster. This isn't lawful or ethical, of course. Beyond that, why risk your reputation on a tax obligation that's insignificant when viewed against the sum of your career?

Above all, inform any part-time employers that your job search is your top priority, and that you can't accept any assignments that would conflict with it. They'll appreciate your candor and probably be willing to structure work that conforms to your schedule.

75.

Are You What You Produce?

You've stepped away from your job search for a few hours to engage in a bit of socializing. You're chatting with a new acquaintance, who turns to you and asks, "What do you do?" Like a morning mist, your good mood evaporates as you realize you must explain once again that you don't do anything right now, that you're hunting for work. The person understands, of course—most people have been down that road—but you feel diminished nonetheless.

If this has happened to you, you've fallen victim to one of society's most pervasive and pernicious misconceptions—that we are no more than what we produce. The corollary, of course, is that if we don't produce anything, we're not very much.

There may have been a time in America when defining people by their jobs made more sense. Before the Industrial Revolution, workers were intimately connected with their work, whether it was tilling the soil, shaping and glazing pots, or crafting furniture by hand. They poured their energy into products that were unique expressions of their personalities and creativity.

Today, many of us labor in bureaucracies that insulate us from actual production. Certainly, we contribute to the development and sale of a product or service, but our hands are among many that help fashion the outcome. In our fast-moving economy, rare is the worker who signs on for a lifetime job. Instead, we change jobs every few years as sectors and trends rise and fall. If we're defined by our work, this mobility will force us to reinvent ourselves with each new job shift.

Your self-image is important, but your job—or the succession of jobs that ultimately will form your career—is only one part of your identity. You are an extraordinary person, a unique blend of traits and talents, experience and expertise, memories and ambitions. You may not be able to convey all of that over cocktails and avocado dip, but it's the complete package that should be front and center throughout your search.

76.

Your Mini-Makeover

A job search usually represents a new phase of your professional life—perhaps your personal life, as well. You'll no longer be in daily contact and partnership with a certain group of friends and colleagues. You won't be driving that old familiar route to work, parking in the same space, and eating in the same cafeteria. Of course, you'll be moving on to many new and exciting friends and adventures. Yet even when we realize the rewarding discoveries that lie ahead, many of us are unsettled by this unsolicited transition.

The problem with lingering in the past is that you won't bring quite the right enthusiasm to your search. So here's an idea to help make the break from your former job a little cleaner. Give yourself a mini-makeover. Not the whole cosmetic transformation that's fashionable these days—that would be costly and unnecessary—but some small yet noticeable physical change.

It could be something as ordinary as a new hairstyle or a more colorful pair of frames for your eyeglasses. If you've never in your life worn anything but full-length neckties, go out and buy a bow tie. If you've been a belt person all your life, outfit yourself with a dashing pair of suspenders. If you've never done much with accessories, experiment with necklaces and bracelets.

Such mini-makeovers have two aspects in common. They're inexpensive, which is a primary consideration during your job search, and they're also quite visible. What you and others will see is someone a little bit different, a little bit livelier than that person who worked in your old job and wore your old clothes.

This is the symbolic break from the past that just could provide a spark to ignite your job search. Each time you catch a glimpse of yourself in the mirror, you'll be reminded that you have the unparalleled opportunity to market this dashing and daring new person.

77.

Keep Setting and Achieving Goals

It's clear that we're much more than we produce on the job, yet work does provide a unique environment for achievement. Every day in the office or on the production line is a day marked by accomplishment. We may not turn out a finished product each day, but we're achieving, nonetheless, by establishing goals and fulfilling them.

During your job search, you're temporarily removed from this crucible of achievement, which can have a discouraging effect. You're not contributing to that team effort anymore, so you may wonder just what it is you *are* accomplishing. Your self-image may seem especially fragile if you're one of those inveterate list-makers. Before, your typical daily to-do list might have had up to two dozen items on it. You gleefully drew a line through each task as it was accomplished; those strokes became symbols of your competence. Now that your list contains only a few items, you may not feel quite that same sense of achievement as you work through your chores.

Unemployment is no reason to slip into drift. You've always been an achiever, and you're *still* an achiever, but now you may need to adjust the focus of your achievements. Your tasks, always job-related before, can assume a more personal and familial nature. Fill up your list with all of those repair jobs that you've been meaning to tackle but never found the time to address. Think about how you can help your spouse, your kids, your parents, and your friends, and add those bullets to your list. How about getting involved with the community? When you volunteer your time for a noble cause, you're achieving in what could be an entirely new and rewarding area.

Once you add these action items to those related to your job search, you'll have a full-bodied list that could even transform you into a more versatile, well-rounded person. You might never have considered family and community involvement items worthy of your to-do list; if you do so now, you'll broaden by far the scope of your achievements.

78.

Don't Be Incommunicado

One of your greatest assets during your job search is your availability. Generally, you can schedule meetings or interviews at the convenience of prospective employers, and you can get back to them in a jiffy whenever they contact you. This won't be the case if you're incommunicado for lengthy periods, so it's a good idea to maintain multiple contact modes.

You may be accustomed to relying on your home telephone as your principal communication tool with potential employers—a fine idea until your spouse and kids need that phone. If you have e-mail and a cell phone as well, you can indicate the appropriate address and phone number on your resumes and job applications so that hiring managers always can reach you. Also, if your home phone doesn't currently offer voicemail, now may be the time to add this feature.

If you do have messaging capability on your phones, make sure to check for messages regularly. This may seem axiomatic, but when a job search turns hectic, it's easy to forget something ostensibly this simple. Consider checking for messages—e-mail, as well—two or three times each morning, and a similar number of times in the afternoon. Make sure your last sweep is before the end of the workday. If you wait until after five in the evening to check your messages and there *is* important news, you may not be able to follow up until the next day. That will provide you with an anxious, sleepless night—just what you don't need.

Even if you've decided to get away from it all for a few days and you're trekking through remote woodlands, someone reliable needs to know where you are and how to reach you—ideally via the cell phone that you're carrying. Your mini-vacation is designed to help you avoid pressure, not job offers. You always want to be informed of those.

If you've been resisting the expense of a cell phone until now, loosen the purse strings a little. Make this investment in your future so that you're always in touch. You'll have an opportunity to reconsider the cell phone when you've landed that great job.

79.

When Reevaluation Makes Sense

As deep as your self-confidence may be, there could come a dark period in your job search that sorely tests your faith. When your hard work isn't yielding interviews, much less offers; when every lead seems a dead end; when your financial resources are dwindling—you may wonder if you're pursuing the right course. This is the perfect time for reevaluation—to assess where you've been and where you think you're going. If you undertake your review in a comprehensive way, it will help you regain any perspective that you've lost in the day-to-day pursuit of work.

Gather together all of your job search materials, including your applications and correspondence from prospective employers. When you lay out all of the documents, they should give you a sense of the patterns that you've followed in your job search. You may discover, for example, that you've been focusing on one business sector at the expense of other potentially promising areas, or that you've been relying too heavily on one tool—classified ads, say, or online vehicles.

With your perspective freshened, you're ready for a pivotal decision. You may decide that you've mined the local territory to exhaustion and that it's time to consider relocation. Alternately, perhaps your abilities don't match up well with availabilities; in that case, skills updating or even a career shift is in order. Then again, your review may convince you that you're on the right track and that success is imminent. Whatever you choose, inform those closest to you. Solicit input from your family, friends, and mentors. They may offer different insights that could help you modify your decision before you finalize it.

Once you settle on a course of action, you'll be ready to pursue it with vigor. The process of reevaluation will be a tonic for your flagging search and energize you all over again.

80.

Dignity Is in You, Not the Job

One of the byproducts of unemployment is a feeling that we lack dignity. This loss of self-esteem is as hazardous as it is unjustified—hazardous because if your confidence is jolted, you may not feel up to the challenges of a job search.

We usually think of dignified people as those who never bend to pressure, who act with integrity and compassion, whose words and deeds always command respect, and who stand tall in the face of adversity. No job is more dignified than any other; in fact, it is people who are dignified, not jobs. Trash collectors can radiate dignity, while high-level CEOs may lack it. Dignity depends on conduct, not commerce. It's earned rather than bestowed.

Our whole notion of dignity needs to be revisited. Your job search is a good vehicle for initiating that process. Keep doing all of the things that your search demands. Never fear that these actions will diminish your standing in the community. The only one who can rob you of your dignity is you—and you won't let that happen.

81.

The Job Fair Scene

When actors audition for roles, they often deride these mass tryouts as "cattle calls," likening themselves to an undifferentiated herd, where personalities and talents aren't perceived as relevant. It's this bit of gentle self-deprecation that keeps them going in the face of long odds and trying times.

If you're not in the acting profession, job fairs may seem to be your equivalent of cattle calls. They're a human stampede of hopeful people showing off a crazy quilt of skills and experience for companies who have never seen them before—and may not be in a hiring mode. When you've tried one or two of these, you may be ready to ride off into the sunset, yet there's ground to be gained here.

Over the past decade, hiring managers have changed their approach to job fairs. When times were flush, companies routinely attended as many job fairs as they could, even if they weren't looking for help at the time. They could flash their fancy booths, earn community relations points with the host town, and realize general goodwill by displaying their names in public. In these cases, job fairs were more image advertisements than recruitment tools.

The softening of the economy forced businesses to spend smarter and attend only those job fairs that might yield a few promising candidates; the corollary public relations benefits became far less important. That's the state of job fairs today, and it means that when you encounter exhibitors, they generally have come to hire.

Look especially for fairs targeted to certain sectors of the economy. Categories include technology, military, sales, professional, health care, and diversity—some will be narrowed down even further. For example, within the broad field of health care, you'll find job fairs dedicated to such specialties as nursing, clinical research, and pharmaceuticals. The great strength of targeted fairs is that exhibitors can rely on an audience with specific interest in that field. Those without the appropriate background are unlikely to attend, so companies and candidates know from the outset that they have something in common. That sets the stage for real dialogue.

Just as employers are more selective about job fairs, you can adopt the same approach. Attend those that seem most likely to yield productive contacts—from companies and fellow job seekers alike. If you feel for a moment like one of the "herd," smile at your own expense—and then mingle.

82.

Who Better to Sell You Than You?

Faced with the challenges of a difficult job search, you might consider bringing on an employment agency to help you market yourself to potential employers. Consultants have something that you may lack—a broad and deep database of professional contacts—so you gain an important asset when you go this route, although you must pay a fee to get it.

You also have something vital that consultants only wish that they had: familiarity with the product—that is to say, with yourself. You appreciate and understand better than any outsider your strengths, your capabilities, your career achievements, and your objectives. In fact, if you put your mind to it, there's no one to sell you any better than you can sell yourself, so why not spend some time promoting this valuable product?

One marketing tool could be a professional or personal portfolio. Your resume will sketch your career highlights; a portfolio can humanize your resume and add some of the supportive details that never could fit in your resume. For example, you might have letters of merit from employers, certificates of commendation from community organizations that you've assisted, or newspaper clippings about important projects that you've led. These can function as the centerpiece of your portfolio.

You can dress up your portfolio with family and work-site photographs. If you apply basic desktop publishing skills to the project, you can fashion a portfolio that's at once informative and reflective of your talents in marketing and design, if those happen to be among your strengths.

How about creating a web site? It doesn't have to be fancy or expensive, but it can offer your resume, your portfolio, professional references, and some innovative features, such as a "thought for the week" that you update regularly. As with portfolios, the benefits of a personal web site are twofold. At one level, prospective employers can gather and absorb key information about you. At a more subtle level, visitors will learn that you're familiar with the tools of technology and that you're industrious enough to use them.

Make sure you that add your web address to your business card. Pass those babies around, and you'll create an indelible first impression.

83.

Be the Best That You Can Be

You may be out of work, but that doesn't mean that you don't have a job. Your mission is to be the best unemployed person you can be—an exemplary "unemployee," if you will. When you're temporarily deprived of the regular schedule that work imposes, you may find yourself slipping into some uncharacteristic bad habits. Since you don't have to be anywhere at any particular time, you might not want to be anywhere at any time. Triggered by the disruption of job loss, a general malaise might take over and stifle progress in the areas of your life beyond work.

This is not at all like you. You've always been an achiever—at times, even an overachiever, reaching for goals even when they seemed beyond your immediate capabilities. How many times have people admiringly called you a "rock," the most reliable person they know? Now is not the time for this rock to crumble. Keep striving, and keep applying your attention and determination to all of your endeavors.

Of course, you'll pursue a new position vigorously and enthusiastically; no one has to remind you of the importance of that. Now bring the same determination to family matters. Resolve to be the best parent, child, and sibling that you can be during this period of potential familial stress. That means sharing the details of your quest with your loved ones, while at the same time allowing them to preserve their private space.

Be the best friend that you can be, as well. Go out of your way to help friends with tasks that easily could be regarded as drudgery. If you're systematic about your outreach efforts, even elevating them to items on your daily to-do list, you'll get that same sense of accomplishment that you used to take home from work.

These exercises really are about maintaining the habits of success. Strong as those habits may be, they're threatened during this strange—perhaps unprecedented—phase of your life, when time, which always seemed so scarce before, looms as a large but intimidating resource. Even if you don't actually need the alarm clock for awhile, set it anyway to help you maintain the rhythm and ritual of success.

84.

Seek the Job or Let It Seek You?

At a retirement party to celebrate the long and notable career of a senior administrator, the guest of honor was asked if he could name his greatest achievement. He responded without hesitation: "I never sought a job. The job always sought me."

At first blush, this may seem a puzzling accomplishment. Most people look for work. Be that as it may, a surprising number of people operate on the same assumption as our distinguished retiree. There may be more at work here than pure ego. Here's how one might analyze the situation. "If I indicate my interest in a job, the employer will know that I want it, know that I need it, and will be able to get me on the company's terms. However, if I'm patient and wait for them to solicit me, they'll know that I have other options—including staying put—so I'll be able to command a better salary and benefits."

There are situations when a coy or even surreptitious job search may be appropriate. Imagine for a moment that you're the CEO of a publicly traded company. If you let it be known that you're looking for work, that could cause confusion or panic among investors, who might rush to dump their shares in the company ahead of what they assume will be a disruption in management. If you work your search quietly, through intermediaries, you can avoid that chaos and harm to your current employer.

It's dreamy to imagine, even for a few seconds, that you might someday work in that rare air where a discreet job search makes sense, but if you haven't reached that lofty pinnacle, most of this high-level gamesmanship won't help much. The equation for most of us is much simpler: If we don't seek positions, how will employers know that we're interested?

So if you've considered resting on your laurels and awaiting suitors, you may be in for a long rest. If a particular position interests you, don't be afraid to pursue it with enthusiasm. Most employers appreciate applicants who show genuine interest in the work. As for the fear that your enthusiasm will result in a less generous offer, you'll have a chance to negotiate those terms when the time is right.

85.

The Numbers Are in Your Favor

Item: The shortage of registered nurses is so acute that by the year 2020, America will have 400,000 fewer nurses than it needs, according to a study published in the *Journal of the American Medical Association*. Shortages by then, projects the Health Resources and Services Administration, will affect forty-four states and the District of Columbia.

Item: In May 2003, the Information Technology Association of America (ITAA) predicted that American companies would seek to fill roughly 493,000 IT jobs in the ensuing twelve months. ITAA considered that a "soft" market, since the personnel need just a few years before was projected as high as 1.1 million.

Item: In Canada, the demand for workers in certain sectors seems just as intense. In 2002, the Canadian Federation of Independent Businesses (CFIB) noted that 265,000 positions at small and medium-sized businesses were unfilled; of those vacancies, 185,000 had been open at least four months.

These are just a few examples of sectors—manufacturing is another—having trouble finding qualified employees to fill availabilities. The figures demonstrate pretty persuasively that even in a down economy, the market is alive with opportunities for people with the right skills—or the hustle to go out and acquire those skills.

If your job search starts to become a grind, these dispatches should offer considerable comfort. Companies *are* hiring; in many cases, they can't hire fast enough. If you haven't matched up yet with businesses in a hiring mode, that's likely to happen soon. Reports such as these also could be a signal that it's time to tweak your skills. Even if you lack the credentials now to apply for an IT position, for example, broadening your talents in that discipline ultimately could make you more attractive to employers who need IT help.

It's only a matter of time before you find a fit between your talents and a company that's eager for those abilities. Keep after it. The numbers are in your favor.

86.

"We'll Keep You on File"

The impersonal nature of job searches can be disheartening. When you don't receive acknowledgment, much less feedback, from the applications that you've submitted or resumes that you've so carefully crafted, you may begin to wonder if this exercise has any point. Sure, you remind yourself that hiring managers are busy, that they're blitzed with resumes and couldn't possibly respond to all of them, that their silence is not a critique of you as a person or candidate. Nevertheless, the frosty climate can chill your momentum.

You certainly don't want that to happen. Here's a fun and different way of preventing it. Keep track of the bland, stock responses that you receive, and rank them based on the annoyance factor. Your list could look something like this.

1) We'll keep you on file. Of all atrocities, this is the worst, since both you and the person who throws this your way know there is no file, or that if a nominal file is maintained, it never will be opened again.

2) We'll get back to you. This one is not necessarily a fabrication, but if they don't give you a time frame for that callback, it sounds suspiciously like a brush-off.

3) That position has been filled. This could be true, but it also could mean that there never was a genuine opening.

4) Thanks for your interest, but... This pro forma rejection tells you nothing about why you weren't selected for the next step.

Once you have responses selected and ranked, you can have some laughs with them—and involve your family, as well. When your kids ask you how things went today, you can tell them, "I got two Number Ones and a Number Three." If you share the experience with loved ones, that will help you maintain an upbeat attitude.

Of course, this type of exercise won't eliminate the pain and disappointment of rejection. Those are real and can't be sugarcoated. However, an inventive sense of humor can allow you to blow off some of your frustrations in a positive way. Now, the stock rejections that are par for this course won't slow you down.

87.

Hitting the Wall

There may come a time in your job search when you come home and announce that you will submit not one more application or subject yourself to one more interview. Distance runners have coined a phrase for that pivotal point in a race where their bodies can't produce enough carbohydrate fuel to keep up with demand and begin burning fat instead; they call it "hitting the wall." You've just hit the job search wall.

If you hit the wall, it's time to step back and regain that positive, can-do outlook. Take a day or a weekend off to do something relaxing and purifying. Don't think about your search while you're enjoying yourself. The idea here is refreshment and renewal.

You should not feel at all guilty about this short vacation. You're simply investing time to rebuild a productive attitude.

When elite runners hit the wall, they find reserves of courage and strength to propel them past their limitations. With only a brief break to help, you'll find those reserves, as well.

88.

Looking While You're Working

One of the stickiest aspects of a job search is looking for work when you're already working full-time. Certainly, no one would deny your right to try to improve your position. Even your current boss, who probably worked somewhere else once upon a time, would recognize that as the American way. However, it is difficult to make time for interviews and meetings with prospective employers when you've committed that time to your current employer.

You can't really request time off to interview for other positions. Few employers are benevolent enough to grant that. Some job seekers resolve this dilemma by taking unauthorized time off work to interview for new positions. This may be the worst solution. In the harshest light, this represents theft of time from your employer. It's unethical, and it can have adverse consequences, as well. If your current employer discovers your subterfuge, you can imagine the response. Try asking that company for a favorable recommendation after you've stolen time from them.

A better approach is to pursue a new position on your own time. Use your lunch hour. Arrange to meet with prospective employers before or after your current workday, or on your days off. Most hiring managers have considerable experience in this sort of thing. They'll go pretty far to accommodate your schedule, particularly since they prefer to hire people who are working rather than unemployed. That's an old HR bias that dies hard.

If you find that you just can't arrange a meeting or interview during one of these times, consider taking a personal day or vacation time to accomplish this task. It's not necessarily the way you want to spend precious time off, but it's better than being deceitful.

You may or may not land the new position that you're seeking, but however it turns out, you'll emerge with your integrity intact. Both your current employer and your prospective employer will appreciate the care that you've taken to be honest. That can only help down the road.

89.

Developing Options

When you're closing in on a job offer, you may be so confident of the outcome and thrilled by the prospects that you shut down all other search-related activities. It's terrific that you've perhaps snared a great position, but there's a risk in ending your search prematurely. If last-minute snags arise, you could be in limbo for a while longer, and it's even possible that this coveted offer won't materialize.

Keep at the search, and you may even develop a number of employment options. Imagine that the job offer you're nearing does come through—but two weeks down the road. You can use that time to pursue other opportunities that may yield still additional offers. That would put you in an enviable position.

Now, you and your family can convene to consider all of the options. One position might offer a greater salary than you earned before but require a numbing commute. A second job would pay you less, but the working conditions and opportunities for advancement seem ideal. A third choice is to consider a career change, a course of action that's always open to you. Yet another option is to reject all of these possibilities if none seems attractive enough, and extend your search.

This is the happiest of dilemmas. Sure, the more options you have, the more challenging it is to select the right one—but you've never lost sight of your most important career and family goals, so choosing the option that best advances those goals won't be that difficult for you.

Think of the great psychological rewards of developing options. Once, you wondered if any employer would want you, and now it seems that every employer wants you. What a lift that is! If you continue to press on with your search, you can proceed with the assurance that you're one hot commodity.

90.

Weighing Your Job Offer

When you score a job offer, you may be so weary of your search that your first inclination is to accept—whether or not it's the right position for you. Even if the prospective employer warns you that they need an answer right away, that's insufficient cause for a rushed decision. You may have other offers pending or just down the road. A career shift and relocation are possibilities for you. You always have the option to keep on searching, too. You're well-positioned to deliberate, weighing the pros and cons, before signing on. Here are some aspects of the offer to consider.

Compensation—salary isn't everything, but your pay should be enough to meet the financial needs of you and your family. If it isn't, is the position so attractive that you can adjust your expenses to make them fit the proposed salary? Think also of bonus potential. Should you and the company both perform well, will you be rewarded appropriately?

Benefits—you'll want to review the entire package, including health coverage, insurance programs, pension plans, and employer contributions to any of these benefits. If vacation is important to you, you need to examine this aspect, as well.

Advancement opportunities—is upward mobility an option? Get a sense of your possible career paths before you find yourself in a dead-end position.

Commute—could you travel to your new work site easily, or would it require a lengthy, exhausting drive or bus trip? Many people don't count time spent commuting as quality time; if you would lose precious quality time just getting to and from work, the offer may not be as spectacular as it looks.

Work conditions—there are many things to contemplate here. Would you work in an office? A cubicle? A large open area? To whom would you report, and do you envision a productive relationship with your supervisor? Employers like to identify "chemistry" in their new hires; you should be probing for that chemistry, as well.

If you find that aspects of the offer aren't up to your expectations, now is the time to negotiate a better deal. Tell the employer what you want; since those in charge of hiring have expressed concrete interest in you, they may be willing to go the final mile to get you.

Chances are that you'll help shape your offer of employment, but if you can't, don't feel guilty about walking away. You've received an offer—this confirms that you're a valuable asset and quite likely to inspire other offers.

91.

Document Your Search

Probably the last thing that you want to worry about is documenting your job search—that is, keeping a record of all the jobs that you applied for, resumes that you submitted, and interviews that you attended. Given the more important priorities of your mission, this can seem like little more than busywork.

However, thorough documentation of what you've done, who you've seen, and what the results were can be helpful in a variety of ways. Perhaps the most immediate reason for documentation is that it will verify your job search for those who administer your unemployment compensation. There's no question that you've earned your compensation, but regulations typically require that you actively search for work to stay eligible for benefits. To be frank, many bureaucracies don't enforce these regulations scrupulously; they may be overwhelmed by the sheer numbers of recipients. Nevertheless, they have the right to require evidence that you're out there hustling work. When you document your search, you have that proof.

Comprehensive records bring other benefits, as well. They'll provide you with a business network that will be an asset, should you need to travel this road again—and you can share this information with friends and colleagues who may be searching for jobs. You'll also be learning a great deal about what certain companies in your region do—what products they make or what services they provide. When you do secure that terrific position and find that you need vendors to serve your new employer, you'll have an excellent list of candidates.

Finally, documentation can verify the validity of your job search in your own eyes. You're aware at some level that you're not idling your time away, but if your search grows long and doesn't produce tangible results, you may begin to question the value of your own activities. That's the right time to pull out your carefully compiled and preserved job search records. You've been working hard to be the best unemployed person you can be—the records prove it.

92.

No Aspect of Your Search Is Futile

One of the features of most job searches is time that's apparently wasted. You've probably made this observation many times yourself: *What a waste of time that interview was. What a waste of time it was responding to that ad. No call back from that company—what a waste of time.*

In terms of the immediate objective—to secure the best position—following dead-end leads may indeed seem like a waste of perfectly good time. Since time is always in short supply on a job search, this is no small thing—yet no aspect of your quest is futile.

Think about all of the knowledge that you acquire during your search. You learn how certain employers operate, even when they don't come through with offers. You learn how to assemble a persuasive and accurate resume. You learn more than you ever wanted to know about interviewing and being interviewed. You learn the finer points of the unemployment compensation system. In short, you become expert in the hiring process. You can deploy all of this newfound information in your career and personal pursuits.

The insights that you gather may be more profound still. As your family "rallies 'round" your job search and you spend more time with them, you'll discover a deeper appreciation of your loved ones. You'll learn new things about your friends, too. A few may offer you superficial help only, but your true friends will be genuinely supportive. You'll appreciate their strengths, and you'll gain the comforting certainty that you can count on them in times of need.

Perhaps most importantly, you'll learn about yourself. You'll uncover talents that may have been hidden before. You'll learn that you have deep reserves of patience and persistence which can be called on in other challenging situations. Your job search is an adventure in awareness. No aspect of it is wasted on your road to security—and enlightenment.

93.

Keep Your Family in the Loop

Including your family in your job search is a must—for your sake and theirs—but how deeply involved should they be? This is one of those tricky balancing acts that everyone in a family situation faces from time to time, made that much trickier because you're dealing with the people closest to you on an emotional subject.

You may opt for a completely open approach and share every detail of your search with your loved ones. At first, they may applaud you for your candor and concern. Soon, though, you may be involving them in every twist and turn of every application, phone call, or interview, until they're subject to the very same pressures that you're enduring. It's bad enough if you're tense, but if they have to ride the job search roller coaster with you, you could end up with a houseful of overwrought folks.

On the other hand, if, in the hope of sparing them, you keep too many of the details and frustrations to yourself, this can be an equally dangerous course. Your loved ones may feel, however wrongly, that you're deliberately shutting them out. Their feelings may be hurt, and they won't be able to pick you up when you're down, since they won't know for sure what's going on. The effect on you can be damaging, as well, if you allow yourself no way to vent any steam to them.

The best approach here may be to share as much of your job search with your family as you can without overloading them. Certainly, if they press you for more information, provide it willingly. Often, just laying out the major themes for them will work wonders. Talking about your quest can help relieve the internal pressure that you're feeling, even as it keeps your loved ones in the loop. When you're hurting, they'll be able to soothe you with sympathy and support. When you're jubilant, they'll be there to celebrate with you, making the occasion even more memorable and unifying.

94.

You're Not Old—You're Wise

If you find yourself looking for work when you're in your fifties, your search takes on a particular urgency. You're well aware that traditionally, employers have shunned older candidates, fearing that they might have to pay a premium for their experience. In any case, why would they hire people only a few years from retirement and then have to endure the recruiting process all over again? Even laws to prohibit age discrimination haven't always been effective against this age-old age bias. However, two trends have combined to deal age discrimination a powerful—perhaps fatal—blow.

When our economy softened in the early years of the twenty-first century, most employers realized that they would have to thin their ranks, yet accomplish just as much as ever, to remain competitive. Who better to help them work smarter than older employees who bring their talent, experience, maturity, and time-honored work ethic to the job every day?

At the same time, we continued to rethink the traditional retirement age of sixty-five and concluded that it was no longer appropriate for all of us, since we were living longer and staying healthier deeper into our lives. If we wanted to work beyond sixty-five, why shouldn't we?

Statistics maintained by the U.S. Census Bureau show the impact of these two potent and intersecting trends. In 2002, seventy percent of Americans between the ages of fifty-five and fifty-nine—more than 10.2 million people—still were active in the noncivilian labor force. More than half of those in the sixty to sixty-four age bracket were part of that workforce. Perhaps most remarkably, more than 13.2 percent of those sixty-five and over remained active, contributing members of our labor force; in 1990, that figure was less than twelve percent.

These numbers suggest that older workers constitute a growing and vital segment on the labor scene, and that employers are fully cognizant of their power. When you launch a job search now as an older worker, you can expect unprecedented receptivity among hiring managers. They no longer see you as old; they perceive you as wise. You're about to show them just how right they are.

95.

Seniors at Work

What jobs are open to older workers? If you pay too much attention to the images that the media often portrays, you may be convinced that seniors in the workforce are stuck in low-pay, low-satisfaction boxes.

Statistics on older workers compiled by the U.S. Census Bureau suggest something quite different. Among workers fifty-five to fifty-nine, more than thirty-six percent were employed in executive, administrative, managerial, and professional jobs in March 2002, compared to more than eleven percent in service categories. For workers in the age range of sixty to sixty-four, thirty-two percent continued in the top classifications; over thirteen percent labored in service occupations. The figures are just as revealing in the sixty-five and older category. Here, nearly twenty-nine percent worked in executive, administrative, managerial, and professional positions, while just more than fifteen percent were employed in the service sector. The numbers tell a persuasive story—if you're an older worker on a job search, the entire range of possibilities is open before you.

If you believe that you need to sharpen your talents or add to your skill base, there's help available from organizations such as Experience Works. Headquartered in Virginia, Experience Works is a national, nonprofit organization that offers training for mature workers in a wide variety of disciplines, including computer skills and technology. Its staffing service places older workers in temporary positions that often lead to full-time employment.

Experience Works also maintains an e-commerce web site—whimsically named Geezer.com—that provides senior artisans and crafters with a market for their wares. Each year, Experience Works reaches an estimated 125,000 mature workers—an indication of how vital these programs are and how enthusiastically they've been embraced.

Other groups—probably some in your region—offer similar services. You may or may not require such assistance, but its availability should help convince you that you remain a valuable commodity in the job marketplace. There's no reason to limit your search to those dreary positions that seem reserved for older workers. Millions of seniors already have demonstrated that they're at home across the breadth of the employment range.

What jobs are open to older workers? Just about all of them, of course.

96.

You're a Valuable Contributor

When you're temporarily without work, you've lost more than just your salary, painful as that blow may be. You also may be missing that sense of being a key contributor to a productive team effort—whether it's creating a product, solving a knotty inventory problem, or pleasing a customer. At the end of a workday, you always could enjoy the satisfaction of looking back on your efforts and knowing that you played a vital role in a common cause. If you're deprived of that role for even a little while, you may begin to question your self-worth.

However, you should be able to see all around you the reasons why you should not do this. You may be off the job for now, but you've mounted an extensive and thorough job search to ensure your family's well-being. That doesn't sound like a person whose worth has eroded.

Your contributions at home are no less crucial there than they've always been. Your family continues to look to you for love and leadership, for advice and approval, for support and strength. You provide all of that, just as you always have. In fact, you dedicate even more time to your family now that your work schedule has eased, so your contributions at home may be greater than ever.

Consider the other aspects of your life, and you'll realize anew what a team player you are. When friends are in need, you selflessly offer to help. When members of your job network feel defeated, you're there to boost their spirits. You're a good neighbor and a force in the community, volunteering your efforts and expertise for a variety of noble causes.

You'll be part of a work team again before long, but look at what you're achieving now. Your professional experience has prepared you to be collaborative and helpful in just about every area of human endeavor, and so you continue to make valuable contributions across the board. You may not be able to succinctly capture this character strength on your resume, but it's a rare and noteworthy accomplishment nonetheless.

97.

Thank You, FELA

Welcome to membership in one of the world's largest clubs—the Formerly Employed League of America (FELA). The membership of this club includes people with an unbelievable roster of skills and strengths. They're faster than a speeding bullet when it comes to problem-solving, they can build a consensus that's more powerful than a locomotive, and they're able to leap over tall challenges in a single bound.

Who are these heroic men and women? For the most part, they're people just like you—those who have lost their jobs but who still bring vast stores of talent and energy to every task. Some FELA members may have higher profiles. Think, for example, of all your supervisors throughout your career. Chances are good that most of them lost a job at one time or another, making them eligible for FELA.

Professional athletes cut by their teams are members, as are most politicians. Virtually every public official has lost an election and been unseated by constituents, meaning that the political sector is well represented in FELA. The ranks also include top business executives rendered superfluous by mergers or acquisitions, actors who fail at auditions, and news anchors whose contracts aren't renewed.

When you think of your situation in this admittedly whimsical way, two things become apparent. The first is that since prestige and a big salary offer limited protection against job loss, unemployment can befall anyone. This realization may take some of the sting from your own dismissal and allow you to view your job search more objectively. When you get beyond the personal element, you're much more likely to be effective.

The second penetrating insight is that business can't do without this collective talent for very long. Employers will turn to FELA members to take up new positions in the competitive wars. When you answer that call, be gracious.

98.

Call Out the Reserves!

The practice of keeping something in reserve is one that we apply to many aspects of our lives. In the area of national security, we maintain a large force of reservists for deployment in military emergencies. In finance, we're accustomed to putting aside a little something for a rainy day. In our homes, we may stock up on nonperishable items as a hedge against bad weather, when trips to the supermarket would be hazardous.

Reserves come in handy on a job search, as well. If the search persists and you don't think that you can endure the grind for even one day longer, it's time to call out the reserves! This is no national emergency, certainly, but it's a personal crisis that demands immediate attention.

You may not think that you have much in reserve, but consider: is there an employment web site that always has a helpful tip, a live opportunity, or even a good joke? If you've been keeping that web site in reserve, now is the time for a visit that will relieve your stress and perhaps get you past your crisis.

How about a trusted friend or mentor who can be counted on for sympathetic yet level-headed advice? Perhaps you've been avoiding contact, because you didn't want to make a pest of yourself. Tap this reserve now. Your friend won't regard you as a nuisance at all, because friends are there for us exactly when we need them.

You may have a special place in reserve, such as a park bench where you can engage in a little people-watching or a mountain top with a spectacular view of the stars. Enjoying these oases too often might make them a little less special, but in this case, you don't want to worry today about what might happen tomorrow. You need your reserves now.

When you reach for that little bit extra, you may find that you *can* go further, and that you are resolute enough to keep searching until you succeed. You'll discover that you have other reserves, as well—of determination and strength.

99.

An Unexpected Breakthrough

We often find something in the last place that we'd think of looking for it. If you've lost your job, finding work can take you down much the same path. You do all of the things that you're supposed to do—compile an eye-catching resume, respond promptly to ads, follow up your interviews—and nothing seems to help. Then, out of the blue, an opportunity emerges that you weren't even aware of, and it leads you to the promised land.

You may consider this fate or luck, yet there's more at play here. You've assembled and deployed a job network that's out there working on your behalf, even when it doesn't appear to be turning up anything concrete. In addition, your search has sensitized you to absorb and react to news that others might not even appreciate as relevant.

In short, the thoroughness and diligence of your search have positioned you for unexpected offers. This is a wonderful result of your hard work, and it means that your breakthrough can come at any time—maybe even from the last place you're looking.

100.

When It All Clicks—and It Will

Ultimately, everything will come together, and your job search will click. You'll be offered an outstanding position that meets your most important needs. When you accept, it will seem that the weight of the world has been lifted from your shoulders. It doesn't matter now what challenges may lie ahead; you've just taken on the toughest assignment that you're likely to face, and you performed admirably. Consider everything that you've achieved.

In a tight job market with thousands—if not millions—of well-qualified people looking for work, you were considered the best candidate for the position that you've just accepted. If your self-esteem was lagging, this verification of your capabilities should relieve any nagging doubts.

You earned this offer the old-fashioned way, through painstaking research, contacts, and follow-up. There were no shortcuts, no favoritism, and no flukes. You got here because you were willing to invest in yourself, whether that meant more time or more money.

You were the architect of a textbook job search—one that you can replicate, should the need ever arise.

The search that you designed and implemented enabled you to widen your cast of contacts. Think about all of the folks that you met while looking for work, whether they were hiring managers who interviewed you or fellow job seekers. While you were establishing these new relationships, you also were reinforcing old ones, as you touched base with friends and mentors.

You picked up even more of value along the way. As you tapped the Internet for opportunities, you were sharpening your online skills to a fine point. Now, you're positively eager for new Internet experiences, and that's likely to be a strong plus in your professional performance. You negotiate the web so smoothly that you can serve as a resource for colleagues still learning how to use it.

How about the fine art of interviewing? Before your search, you may have found interviews intimidating, whether you were the interviewer or the subject. At this point, you're a veteran of the mahogany table. You know how to respond to questions productively, and you know how to conduct interviews with candor and compassion—because it was precisely those qualities that so often were lacking in those who grilled you.

In a word, your job search has enriched you. You're more confident, more skilled, and more empathetic than when you began this journey. Your destination was important—and so, it seems, was how you got there.